THE
PERSONAL
BRANDING
PLAYBOOK

THE
PERSONAL BRANDING PLAYBOOK

TURN YOUR PERSONALITY INTO YOUR COMPETITIVE ADVANTAGE

AMELIA SORDELL

CAPSTONE
A Wiley Brand

Registered Offices
John Wiley & Sons, Inc., 111 River Street, Hoboken, NJ 07030, USA
John Wiley & Sons Ltd, The Atrium, Southern Gate, Chichester, West Sussex, PO19 8SQ, UK

For details of our global editorial offices, customer services, and more information about Wiley products visit us at www.wiley.com.

Wiley also publishes its books in a variety of electronic formats and by print-on-demand. Some content that appears in standard print versions of this book may not be available in other formats.

Library of Congress Cataloging-in-Publication Data is Available

ISBN 9780857089830 (Paperback)
ISBN 9780857089854 (ePDF)
ISBN 9780857089847 (ePub)

Cover Design: Wiley
Author Photo: © Stacey Clarke

Set in 10.5/16pt and Plantin Std by Straive, Chennai, India
SKY10092922_120424

This book is dedicated to anyone and everyone who has ever had the audacity to be 100% OK with the consequences of being themselves, both online and off.

Note from the Author

When my Editor asked me to find the most famous person I knew to write the Foreword of this book, I stalled. It didn't feel right to me. And maybe because a foreword by a 'famous person' is what every other author does – and as you'll find out as you begin to read this book, I don't like convention very much.

I also think that 'famous people' don't benefit from what I teach. They've already built their brand and made their name. They're already basking in the abundance of opportunities that being themselves delivers. And that isn't who this book is for. This book is for people like you and me. People who are ambitious and smart and who deserve opportunities but don't quite know how to get them. Yet.

So instead of having a 'famous person' write my foreword to superficially impress you, I have included a collection of endorsements from friends, clients and community members who have been touched in some way by my work and the principles I teach in this book. People who wanted more, and who followed what I teach and have achieved it.

These people are freelancers, CEOs, founders, marketers, social media managers, finance bros, accountants and students. They're regular people, who want more than just a regular life. And if you get half the amount of value they have from the contents of this book, the 12 months it's taken me to write it will be worth it.

Praise for *The Personal Branding Playbook*

"Amelia is one of the very few people who inspired me on LinkedIn to start posting more and build my own personal brand as I wouldn't have bothered or be where I'm at with it today. She's a force for greatness!"

Dan Murray-Serter, Founder and CEO Heights
and Host of the Secret Leaders podcast

"There are so many ways Amelia's content has ultimately transformed me into becoming my own unapologetic boss today. And, for that, I appreciate her."

Alicia Richardson, Founder and CEO of Create Connect

"*The Personal Branding Playbook* delves deep into the principles of personal branding, sharing invaluable insights and practical advice. Her journey, marked by bold decisions and unwavering authenticity, is a powerful testament to the impact of a solid personal brand."

Elfried Samba, Co-founder and CEO of Butterfly 3ffect
and ex-Gymshark Head of Social (Global)

"I have watched and subscribed to many influencers over the years and tried to be brave and learn to raise my profile. I know what I'm good at, but I need more confidence in selling myself. Then I came across Amelia's profile, and things changed for me. How she comes across as just who she is, a real person, but also someone knowledgeable and professional in every scenario has taught me that people take less notice if you try to be someone you are not. I am using every piece of advice that you offer, and it's working! Thank you, Amelia, for the tips, hints, and content."

Maria Moulton, Founder of Willow Consulting

"Amelia is the poster girl of personal branding and self-confidence."

Harry Hugo, Co-founder of The GOAT Agency

"Amelia is the queen of personal branding. I always had this vision of building a personal brand but was reluctant as it's hard to put yourself out there. Amelia helped me bring out my true self and have confidence. As she says . . . just f*cking post it."

Jonny Sitton, Co-founder and CEO of My 1st Years

"Amelia is a force of nature, she has shown LinkedIn and the rest of the internet the power of personal branding. If her content doesn't show you this already, then let Amelia teach you how to cultivate, elevate and motivate your personal brand with *The Personal Branding Playbook*."

Hannah Holland, Founder and CEO of HLD Talent

"Amelia has opened my eyes to the incredible power personal branding has not only for you as an individual but also for your organisation as a whole. She is a canny business professional and fearless innovator."

Jeremy McLellan, Head of Learning & Development,
EMEA Alvarez and Marsal

"I used to have a crippling fear of failure and nearly gave up on my business because of it. Then I saw a video of Amelia openly sharing her biggest mistakes and being unapologetically herself. That moment changed my perception of failure. I stopped trying to be someone I wasn't and embraced who I truly am. Within three months, my business grew, and people wanted to work with us because of our authenticity. And that changed my life."

Breanne Jones, Founder of Soleil Media

"Mine and Amelia's journey started out with me as her client, but she fast became an integral part of my most treasured inner circle. Whilst her authenticity, expertise and impact are both obvious (and otherworldly), for me, Amelia's signature qualities are her humanity, generosity, and humility – things *The Personal Branding Playbook* delivers in spades."

Jordan Barry-Bayliss, former FTSE CPO,
Consultant and Executive Coach

"What I love about Amelia is her no BS approach. She'll tell you straight (in real life or on LinkedIn) – and if she doesn't have the answer, she will still be there to champion you. Amelia's the confidence hype woman we all need."

Sedge Beswick, Exited Founder and Consultant

"Amelia inspired me to use my challenges as a first-generation student and turn them into a helping hand for millions of college students across the globe. It is also thanks to her that I expanded my comfort zone and have had the opportunity to speak at events, network with other professionals, and become a leader on campus. I feel blessed to have such a strong female entrepreneur to look up to as I continue my multifaceted career."

Katie Goble, Marketing Degree student
and Founder of Your College Big Sister

"Within my first 90 days of following Amelia's principles, I saw a significant increase in the reach of my LinkedIn content, our podcast downloads increased globally, I've been booked for speaking and training engagements and I've started coaching other administrative assistants alongside my day job. These achievements are no coincidence. To Amelia – thank you for showing me what's possible, how to achieve it, why it matters, and how to remain accountable and focused to see real change and results."

Jodie Mears, C-Suite Executive Assistant
and Co-host of The Crodie Files podcast

"I was fresh on the start-up scene and Amelia was the first female business owner I had met. I remember coming away feeling utterly gobsmacked by how she spoke, presented herself, backed herself – all the traits she has are ones I have always admired. We were chatting openly about how it's going, my own personal branding, and I was so overwhelmed by Amelia's nature to just help – no strings attached. Since that first meeting, we've shared notes, ideas, headaches, and Amelia has always made it abundantly clear that whatever I need, whenever I need it, she's there. In this day and age in the professional world, that might be the rarest of all traits. I'm so proud of her for this brilliant book."

Vic Banham, CEO and Director of Antler Social

"Let me tell you about Amelia Sordell. Maybe I can share some things that you won't know from reading the other endorsements in this book and taking a look online at her social media accounts. Amelia is a force of nature, with infectious enthusiasm for personal branding and the ability to convince even her online trolls to become her biggest fans through her persistent kindness and witty comebacks. I have been fortunate enough to spin in her orbit as her Executive Assistant for the last four years (sometimes I'm the one keeping everything IN orbit, but that's an entirely different book). It's a privilege to call Amelia not only my exec, but also my friend. She has taught me an awful lot about the power of personal branding (and now she's going to share that with all of you), but she's also taught me lessons in resilience, humility, and owning your f**k-ups and mistakes too. I hope you enjoy this book as much as I enjoy working with the human being behind it. She really has poured her heart into it."

Amy Lester, EA to Amelia Sordell
and Founder of Typing and Tasks Virtual Assistants

"Amelia holds a unique view on having built both her own brand to a huge audience and being a practitioner for others. She does what is so often lacking in business by telling it how it is and I've no doubt her words and advice can help countless others on their journey."

Ash Jones, Personal Brand Strategist and Founder
of Great Influence

"Since the day I met Amelia, before her epic rise as a business leader and personal branding expert, she has always been 100% authentically herself. Amelia is the same person online and offline, and if you're looking to build your personal brand the right way, look no further than *The Personal Branding Playbook*."

Daniel Murray, Founder of Authority & The Marketing Millennials

"Amelia's fearless spirit and audacious approach to life have been a constant source of inspiration, empowering me to embrace bravery and boldness in everything I do, from personal branding and business ventures to the quiet moments of my personal life."

Sophie Miller, Founder and Director of Pretty Little Marketer

"Amelia is the rare marketer who is both style and substance. She and her company have been at the forefront of the personal branding movement and she has a deep understanding of both the optics and tactics that lead to success. Her confidence rubs off on everyone she interacts with and this book can be a game-changer for those wanting to start or build on their personal brand."

Oz Rashid, Chief Executive Officer,
MSH Talent & Technology Solutions

"I have been working with Amelia for nearly a year now and have increased my following by nearly 100% during that time across all channels. However, as she says, following is vanity – it's about the engagement. I now have an ever-growing engaged audience which has really helped me propel my own brand and that of my business. Very happy with all of the work Klowt and Amelia have done!"

Chris Ball, Managing Partner, Hoxton Capital Management

Contents

Acknowledgements

I put the word 'Book' on my list of life goals in 2018, and in September 2023 I signed the deal with Wiley to publish The Personal Branding Playbook. None of this would have been possible without you. I started posting content online in 2018, and without you I would not have the platform I have, and the voice I have to share my story both here and online – I thank you. From the bottom of my heart. For your support, your kind words, your challenging ones too. Without you, this book, nor the career I love, would be possible. Which leads me to my children. My hilarious, confident, kind and slightly feral children. The countless hours you have spent in after-school clubs. The missed sports days, plays and performances have not gone unnoticed. You never complain, you're never upset with me for missing some of your milestones and your unwavering support of Mummy's dreams have inspired me even more to be the best mother, author and human being I can be. I love you.

To my mother, Louise, for your endless love and support. Your rose-tinted glasses were just the tonic I needed when I was about ready to give up. To my father, Meyrick, for teaching me that everyone deserves the right to their opinion. Even if it's wrong. To my brother, Elliot. To ensure that throughout my 'successes', my head stays firmly on my shoulders, in the version of humility that only a sibling can provide.

To my closest friends and chosen family, Elisha Warburton, Victoria Rush, Madeline Connolly, Nicola Scott-Douglas, Claire Dickson-Bahl and Charlotte Mair. To be surrounded by inspiring, dedicated, hard-working powerhouses of women is a honour. Thank you for loving me, supporting me and pushing me to follow my dreams, even when it meant that I missed some of the big and small moments in your life. Your friendship will be cherished forever.

To my partner Nick. For being my greatest support, biggest cheerleader and the ultimate hype man If I came home and told you I wanted to be an astronaut, I know that you'd help me figure out a way to get on the moon.

To Amy Lester, my executive assistant, confidante, friend, support and CEO of my life. I cannot function without you, least of all attempt to write a book. You juggle my chaotic life and schedule with a newborn baby on your hip and make it look easy. You're an inspiring mother, woman and friend. I can only hope to be even a little bit like you when I grow up.

To my long-suffering team: Danielle Mimoni, my first employee, for putting up with my s**t for as long as you have and for always being game for 'giving it a go'. To Liam Jones, one of the the only men in the world who's has figured out a way to keep me in line. To Megan-Eve Hollins for your loyalty and support and for joining me on the many wild adventures and side quests I have taken us on over the years in pursuit of growth. To Hannah Emery, Delia Rowland, Daniel Shale, Oliver Wright, Samuel Spencer, Tarek Ahead – Klowt's first intern and my eternal hype man - for being the most incredible team I could ever hope to have. You make coming to work a fun, enjoyable and fulfilling experience. It's real honour and privilege to get to work alongside you. To Leah Matthews. We've worked together for ten years, and finally in 2024 you decided, perhaps regretfully, to join our team full-time. Your pragmatic, balanced and truly inspired approach to brand management inspires me every day. This book, its cover and my brand wouldn't be what they are without you.

To Ivan Meakins, the project manager and content strategist, who extracted the information we needed from me to be able to write this book – and did such a good job of it, I convinced you to come and work for me at Klowt. Thank you. I am forever indebted to Annie Knight and Alice Hadaway and the entire team at Wiley, thank you for believing in me enough to give me the chance to write this book. It is because of your efforts, encouragement and positivity throughout this process – even when I was not at all positive – that this book has even reached the printing press. Writing a book about how I changed my life is a surreal process. And so much harder than I imagined, but so much more rewarding than I ever thought imaginable. It is an honour to get to share my story – and I hope that it inspires your own.

Introduction

Building my branding changed my life. I don't just mean it changed my working life. I mean it changed every part of my life. For the better. In some ways, personal branding saved me – it helped me reconnect with who I was and what I loved at a time when, in all honesty, I was lost.

Before building my personal brand, I was getting paid OK, I guess. But I was working a job that I didn't love and as a result every day felt like a negotiation with myself to get out of bed. Every day felt like a struggle. I was living pay cheque to pay cheque. I lacked focus, I lacked vision and I lacked the confidence to even know where to start. I had a job that I didn't enjoy. I didn't own my own home. My marriage was coming to an end. I was struggling, mentally and physically. I was so focused on making sure my family was OK, that I forgot about myself. I forgot myself. At times I remember asking myself, *Is this really what I'm going to do for the rest of my life?* Little did I know, a door was about to open for me – all I had to do was walk through it.

It all started one otherwise uneventful Tuesday. I had taken a role heading up B2B marketing at a recruitment agency I worked for when I returned from maternity leave. This meeting was between myself, the B2C Marketing head, and the Chief Commercial Officer. Despite the bland walls in the meeting room and standard-issue conference table, I vividly recall every detail of our discussion.

We were talking about the business' marketing strategy for the next four months, and where we wanted marketing to sit within the business as a whole. Contrary to popular belief, those of us in the marketing department are not only there to 'jazz up presentations'. Marketing should always drive revenue, and should be measured in those terms. How we, as the marketing department, could do that was the purpose of our meeting.

We ate sushi, talked tactics and reviewed the data from the last year. It became obvious very quickly that, while we'd always focused much of our efforts (and budget) on marketing the company brand, the majority of our new business and the candidates who applied for the roles we were working on came to the business because they liked individual recruiters, NOT because they liked our brand name. That's not to say the company brand was bad, on the contrary, it had a good reputation, but we kept seeing the same pattern – our clients liked us for our people, not for our company name.

In a service-based business, your people are your product. So, to me, the solution was simple: why spend time and money marketing the brand when we could instead market our people and, by proxy, market the brand? It was actually easier to market the people because they were the ones delivering the product we were selling. And they did a damn good job of it. We presented our idea to the CEO. . . who thought it was nonsense. His main objection was that if our recruiters advertised how good they were at their jobs, they would get poached by our competitors. My objection to his argument was that if our recruiters got poached, that said more about us as an employer than it did about the recruiters posting online. We got our answer, though, it was a resounding 'no'.

But I couldn't let it go. I knew it would work – I should probably tell you at this point that if there's a big red button that says 'Do not press', I'm the kind of person who will press it. I'm more of an ask for forgiveness than ask for permission girl, you know? So, I decided

I'd start building my personal brand online. In truth, I only started posting content online to prove my CEO wrong. But what happened next changed my life forever.

Putting myself out there

I decided to focus on LinkedIn because that's where the company's audience was. In a little under four months, I went from having 1,500 followers to having about 13,000. I posted about marketing, employee engagement, leadership and how to be a better employer. These were all topics I knew about, and crucially were topics I knew would resonate with the audience I was trying to attract. But beyond that, I had no clear strategy. I just paid attention to what worked and what didn't, what people seemed to like and what they didn't seem to like, but the resounding feedback I received was that people seemed to enjoy reading what I was posting.

I realised it wasn't necessarily because *I* was saying these things, but because someone, an actual human, was saying them. My plan had worked. Marketing myself had brought more engagement than any other marketing tactic we'd tried as a business. I knew I was sitting on something powerfully unique: my personality. This was when I decided to double down and get more intentional and consistent in what and how I posted. I started recording videos about topics that had already done well as written posts. I'd record them while I was out walking my dog in the morning. I'd set up a makeshift tripod out of stacked books and share videos about employer branding, engagement and posting content on LinkedIn.

I'm not going to pretend this came naturally to me. I felt uncomfortable putting myself out there. I often felt incredibly insecure about what I was posting. In the early days I would spend hours perfecting a single post. I was scared of people judging me, or thinking I was stupid. I was scared of doing it wrong. It sounds ridiculous now to think back to the amount of time I must have spent debating whether I should use the word 'amazing' or 'fantastic' in a post, but the reality is, like maybe even you, I had crippling anxiety about people judging me.

And, of course, the more I posted, the more often I got the occasional comment from people disagreeing with me – whenever I saw one of those, my stomach sank. It felt like being back at school and not feeling good enough. It was horrendous. But I pushed through. When I look back now, I wonder why I cared so much about what 'Steve from Colchester' thought. No offence to Steve, or to Colchester (I don't know why I always use Steve and Colchester as the example to prove this point) but these were people I was never going to meet in real life and, let's face it, if we did meet, would have zero bearing on whether or not my life was successful.

You'll be pleased to know that although I do get those pangs of fear associated with rejection from time to time, the more I've posted, the less I've cared what Steve or anyone else thinks. I know my heart, I know my value. I actually quite like it when people don't agree with me now – it's a good opportunity to learn something new (or prove someone wrong). Maybe you're feeling that anxiety while you stare at the 'post' button, wondering if you should. You might even be feeling it right now as you read this book. I hear you and I've been there, but you can push through to the other side where a world of opportunity – and the freedom to be unapologetically yourself – wait. This book is going to show you how.

Now, I wish there was a sexier solution to the problem we all have with fear – but the reality is you just have to keep at it. Think of building your personal brand like training at the gym to get the sexiest body of your life. It won't happen overnight. There will be pain, self-doubt and times when you don't want to be at the gym along the way. But you know that if you want to see those abs, you have to keep going – you can't jack it in after four weeks because you weren't 'seeing any results'.

What I will say about building confidence in yourself is that confidence comes from being OK with being told you're wrong, not from always feeling like you're right. That was one of the lessons I learned during this period. Despite my anxiety around people not liking my content, my following continued to grow and after six months, I had 18,000 followers. I had also started receiving messages from people asking me how I'd done it.

'How did you get all those followers? Can you give us some tips?' was a very common theme in my inbox. I pivoted and started sharing more content about how to build a personal brand on LinkedIn and why it was such a powerful thing to do.

I was also incredibly lucky that I started doing this at a time when LinkedIn was desperate for more people to post content. I saw it as an opportunity and treated it like a giant conference where I could get myself in front of people that I thought would positively impact my career in some capacity. Only the impact didn't come in the form I'd expected.

A new door opens

The more I succeeded in building my personal brand on LinkedIn, the more I felt I was taking back control of my life and moving away from being in a victim mentality. I believe that sometimes God (or whatever higher power you believe in) gives you a door and it's up to you to choose to ignore it and stay in the crappy situation you're in, or to walk through it. There have been many doors I haven't walked through in my adult life, because I was comfortable where I was, even if I was also miserable. Maybe the misery was comfortable, because it was predictable.

But this time a door appeared when I not only felt miserable in my job, but also miserable in my relationship – I didn't feel comfortable anywhere in my life. The door in question was a job offer from a private equity firm. Ironically, despite proving to my old CEO that my approach worked, I also proved him right about his fear of other businesses poaching our talent. . . if only he'd listened to me about being a supportive employer.

Joe Curtis, the CEO of 11 Investments (a private equity company that invests in recruitment companies), reached out to me. 'Hey, Amelia, I've been following you for a while and I don't know what you're doing but it's amazing. Can we have a conversation? We're looking for a head of marketing and we think you might be a good fit.'

That was my door. I didn't hesitate to open it. I met Joe, went through the company's whole interview process, and gave a presentation about what I proposed they do for their marketing strategy. It was between me and one other person for the role. And they chose the other person.

Don't feel bad for me, though. Joe liked me so much, he offered me a job anyway. He said to me he didn't know what my role would be yet, but that we'd figure it out when I arrived. So, I handed in my notice at the recruitment agency I was working for, found a house in London and moved to a new city with my then-husband, two-and-a-half-year-old daughter and nine-month-old son. It was 2019.

I arrived at the 11 Investments office on my first day, ready to get started. I walked up to reception, 'Hi, who are you here to meet?' they asked.

'I'm Amelia, it's my first day. I'm here to start a new job with you.'

'Oh, what are you here to do?'

'I don't actually know. . .' It turned out that Joe hadn't told anyone he'd hired me. The Operations Manager had no idea who I was. I had no laptop, no desk, no job title and no job description. This was, with hindsight, the best thing that could have happened. My official job title ended up being Employee Engagement Manager, but I did so much more than this.

I did everything from recruitment marketing, event organising and employee engagement to marketing for other recruitment agencies and teaching the founders in the portfolio how to build their personal brands. In many ways, it was madness, but the amazing thing about this role was that I was involved in budgeting, headcount analysis, profit and loss, calculating costs and working out pricing for products and services. What a door to have walked through – I'd landed in a real-life MBA programme that taught me how to start, build and grow a profitable business. And got paid to do it.

Sparking my entrepreneurial spirit

I've been a cookie-cutter entrepreneur my entire life. I used to charge my parents 20p for a hand massage. I managed to convince my Dad to pay me for every A I got in my exams. I've always had a hustle but it's never really been about the money for me. What I love is finding ways to win at the game of building something – money is just a tangible outcome of that.

I set up my first business when I was 22, and not long out of university. I'd spent a year working for an event sales agency, but I picked up sales very quickly and so by the end of a year there, I was bored of the role and looking for a new challenge. That was when I decided to quit my job and start a fashion brand.

Using YouTube videos, I taught myself how to set up an ecommerce shop, how to do product shoots, how to do PR – I even got myself into publications like *The Daily Mail* – and how to use influencer marketing. Coleen Rooney and Danielle Lloyd were among my clients. Year one, I was profitable. My clothes were stocked in 12 different boutiques, internationally, and ASOS was courting me to stock my brand on their platform.

In year two, I lost everything. I made some bad business decisions. But the thing that ultimately sunk me was receiving a large order for some very expensive products from an ecommerce store that, between placing the order and paying for the stock, ceased to exist. The way it works in a fashion retail business like mine is that the stores would pay 30% upfront for the next season's collection, which covered manufacturing costs, and the remainder on delivery.

All of a sudden, I was left with $85,000–$100,000 worth of stock that I couldn't shift. The other boutiques I worked with had already placed and received their orders for that winter, and I didn't have enough traffic going to my website to sell the volume of stock that was in my spare bedroom. All my money was tied up in those clothes – so, I didn't have any money to run the business. Or pay myself.

I was left with a choice. I could either take out a huge loan, which I would have to personally guarantee, or liquidate the business. As a 20-something year old with no real understanding of business or of how finance worked, I was scared. And so, I chose to liquidate the business. Closing that business down felt like death. I had tied my entire identity to being the Managing Director of my business. It was a very humbling experience, because it made me realise I didn't know everything – looking back, I needed to be humbled. My ego had meant I'd made bad decisions because I thought I had it all figured out – but that didn't make it any easier at the time.

That was how I started and left entrepreneurship – and it's also how I ended up in recruitment at 11 Investments. But when I left that business behind, I always felt as though my failed fashion brand wouldn't be my only stab at running a business.

So, back to 11 Investments. I was learning a lot. I was fortunate enough to be working for a man named Joe Curtis. Joe's management style was very much a case of leave you to get on with it, and under his wing I had the freedom to try and test, to post content and to inspire others in the business to do the same. I learned how to scale a service-based business, he showed me how to run a profit and loss (P&L) and how to charge properly (and make a profit). He taught me how to run a company – and built my confidence. By the time the COVID-19 pandemic hit in 2020, I felt ready to become an entrepreneur again. I had the skills, I just needed an idea.

All change

While many of the employees at 11 Investments were furloughed during the pandemic, I continued working. And as the world went online and my personal brand skyrocketed, I was receiving more and more messages from people asking how I'd managed to get so many followers on LinkedIn. After mentioning this to Joe, he suggested we sell online personal branding workshops to recruitment agencies, which I could create and deliver. I've told a lot of people about this arrangement since and they all respond the same way: 'You did all that extra work and didn't get paid?!' No, I didn't get paid additionally for creating and running those workshops – 11 Investments did. But it also meant I was on a full-time salary and was able to test a model of 'personal branding' workshops to see if it could work as a business. I got paid to test out my business plan. And the business plan worked.

I'd worked out a great format of delivering these workshops and had begun to build a bit of a reputation as 'the' person to train recruiters. I was getting a handful of inbound leads a week and by August 2020 handed in my notice to Joe and 11 Investments to set up Klowt. I officially registered the business on 31 July, but didn't start the business properly until Monday 8 August. I had my first two clients by the Thursday of that week – all thanks to my personal brand.

Going from strength to strength

Within the first six weeks of launching Klowt, I was oversubscribed. As in, my personal brand was so strong that as soon as I announced what I was doing, I had people queuing up to work with me. I had made the biggest problem most businesses face – generating business – disappear, all through my personal brand.

And by the end of those first six weeks, I'd hired my first employee. I simply couldn't manage the demand by myself, and so hired a part-time social media executive to help me stay on top of things. It wasn't long after that I was asked to be on a virtual panel at the Influencer Marketing Show – one of my first proper speaking gigs. Since then, I've done dozens of keynotes, been asked to speak at LinkedIn HQ twice and get paid to be on panels, webinars and stages around the world, talking about how employers, founders and individuals can leverage personal brands to gain a competitive advantage.

We were flying. And by February 2021, Klowt and our little two-person team had moved into our first office. Five months later, after outgrowing our six-person office, we moved into a shared space in Soho, London. Ten months after that, we moved to another larger space in Covent Garden. Then New Bond Street and now Chancery Lane. Every move, while stressful, has signalled a reminder of how incredible this journey has been – and a reminder that we've managed to hire, train, build and develop a team of 15, all off the back of my and my teams' personal brands. At the time of writing this book, we have generated nearly $1 million in revenue off the back of my personal brand. In less than three years, I went from feeling trapped, miserable – completely and utterly out of control of my life and my future – to holding my destiny and every single opportunity I've ever had in my hands.

Which leads me to you. Being asked to write this book has been one of my life's greatest achievements. I am so grateful and feel so humbled to have the opportunity to share what I believe is a life-changing secret with you. To help you uncover what you want, who you really are, and share that person with the world, unapologetically. I hope that by sharing my journey and everything I've learned, you too will understand the power of your personal brand, and the impact it will have not just on your professional life, but on your personal life too.

I have always wanted to write a book. But I'd never believed a publisher would care enough to publish it. I have nothing against self-published books, I was resigned to the fact that I would be a self-published author. And so when I got the email from Annie at Wiley about writing and publishing this book, it was yet another example of the impact of building your personal brand.

Annie had been following me on LinkedIn for a while. She was impressed with how honest, open (and popular) my content was. She said she'd be speaking with her editors in the US and asked if I'd be interested in speaking about writing a book.

Being contacted by a publisher was surreal, but also a validation of how powerful everything I'd been doing was.

Until that moment, I'm not sure I'd really believed I was worthy of sharing this message – and in all honesty, I still find it astonishing that anyone cares what I have to say online. I get paid to speak about personal branding on stages to hundreds, sometimes thousands of people. I work with executives on the boards of some of the biggest companies in the world. And, even though you're holding my published book in your hands, reading this right now, I still have moments of self-doubt. The difference between the woman I introduced you to at the beginning of this book, and who I am now, is I don't see that as a bad thing.

I think people can look at people with large followings and strong opinions and believe that they have something they don't: confidence and self-belief. The reality is that, no matter what you achieve in life, you always have self-doubt. The difference is that I, and so many people I have looked up to, know that self-doubt is what keeps you competitive. It's what keeps you – and your ego – from getting lost in the sauce of success. It also makes sure that you never lose sight of what this is all for. One thing I'm acutely aware of after the failure of my first business is that I will never know it all – and thinking that you do is when you lose everything.

So embrace self-doubt. Embrace the opportunity to fail. Know that the difference between building a strong personal brand, and not, is your ability to tolerate and move through times when you're not good enough at something or you fail.

I am thankful for every failure, every mistake, every post I shared that got one like and for every missed pitched or forgotten word on stage, because without those I wouldn't have a job I love. Without embracing the opportunity to be wrong, my life wouldn't feel so right.

It's time to take control of your life, starting with your personal brand

Helping you build your personal brand isn't the reason I've written this book. It's helping you change your life and attract every single opportunity you've ever wanted.

The way I see it, your personal brand is everything. It's your reputation, your resume, your gateway to attracting life-changing opportunities into your lap and ultimately reaching your potential.

By the end of this book, you will have all the tools and tactics you need to build your personal brand, but know that the real power in heading on this journey comes from understanding that it's not about posting content, or speaking on stages, or even publishing books. It's about being recognised as who you really are, taking control of your life and your future – and changing its trajectory as a result.

Taking control of your personal brand and reputation is taking control of what you want your life to look like. It's about becoming accountable for your own success.

I always say, if you don't want to drown, learn how to swim. Personal branding teaches you how to swim and also sends you a speedboat that comes with champagne on board for good measure.

One of the most rewarding things about what I do is being able to inspire others to believe in themselves to take action, build their brand and change their lives forever. I was working out recently with my trainer, Paul. I was a sweaty mess, hair scraped back, panting (and probably sweating) like a pig, when a woman approached me. I thought she was coming to ask to take the equipment we'd been using, instead she asked, 'Hi, are you Amelia Sordell?' My brain went into overdrive. *Where the hell do I know this woman from?* I nodded and smiled at her, while mentally trying to place her. She broke into a big grin.

'I've been following you on LinkedIn for the last 18 months and I just wanted to say thank you because you've inspired me so much – because of you, I've quit this to start that and I just wanted to say, I would never have done that had I not seen you talking about the times you'd screwed up and where you are now. So, thank you so much, and keep sharing the message you're sharing.'

I was smiling, but speechless. I managed to say, 'You're welcome', before she headed off to start her gym session. I turned to look at Paul, with tears in my eyes. He was beaming at me. 'That's amazing,' he said.

It is amazing. That kind of feedback is the reason I do what I do. That is why I'm writing this book. What I want you to take from it, and any of my other content, is that you are so much more capable, confident and amazing than you believe you are. You can achieve anything you want, all you have to do is take control, walk through the doors that open for you and remember that not every closed door is locked, so push!

Building your personal brand will help you get the job you've always wanted, get the pay rise you know you deserve, will help you generate the leads your business needs, the talent your team has to have, attract contacts into your network that your professional and personal life needs. By starting the process of taking control of your life and building your personal brand, you're going to shine a light on all the things you've been too afraid to share, too afraid to do. It will feel uncomfortable, but stick with it. That's where the magic happens.

I have been on this journey for nearly five years and I'm still on it. I can't tell you how life-changing building my personal brand has been. Before, I felt like I was floating – like I had no direction, that I wasn't rewarded for the work I was doing and that the work I was doing wasn't meaningful. I didn't feel as though my life was going anywhere.

Now, I have had the courage to quit my job and start a business, which I've grown and scaled to one generating more than $1 million in revenue. I've hired an incredible team. I've spoken at LinkedIn twice. I've launched a podcast and appeared on nearly one hundred as a guest. I own my home outright, and can take my children on holidays I would never have thought I would be able to afford. I've made amazing friends. I have the opportunity to do whatever I want, when I want, with whoever I want. That is the true definition of freedom – and that is why I am not exaggerating when I say personal branding has changed my life. Now it's time to change yours.

THE PERSONAL BRANDING PLAYBOOK

1

Reputation at scale

I went on a date with this guy. Picture me at a nice restaurant, there's delicious food on the table and sitting opposite me is an attractive man. We met online and now, a few days after we matched, we met for dinner. So, I'm on this date. He's chatting away, we are getting on well. He's handsome, attentive; seems to have his stuff together. He's a real gentleman. . . to me.

About halfway through our main, the waitress appears to refill our rapidly disappearing glasses. As she does, I make a point to make eye contact and smile as I say, 'Thank you'. She smiles back, gives a brief nod and then retreats to the edge of the restaurant. I know that she's watching for when she'll next need to provide us with a top-up or a dessert menu. She's been brilliant all night.

Then it hits me. Not once has the guy opposite me acknowledged her presence, let alone thanked her for anything. For the rest of the night I'm very aware of how he behaves around the waitress. As we get ready to leave, our waitress brings our coats from the cloakroom. He takes his from her without a word, but she beams at me as she hands mine over. 'Thank you so much for such a wonderful evening', I say as I button up my coat.

I'm talking to the waitress, not my date.

This is a true story. (Spoiler: we did not see each other again.) The reason I am telling you it is because your personal brand is built with every interaction you have. Every person you meet forms an opinion of you and your character. That not only means people who are your clients, employees and colleagues in your professional life. You also have a personal brand with the barista you buy your coffee from and the taxi driver who drops you off at the station and the shop assistant who helps you find an alternative size and your date to a nice restaurant. In reality, you do not build your personal brand, you take control of it.

I share a lot of content about being 100% OK with the consequences of being yourself, about not caring what people think about your opinions. But I care deeply about how other people perceive my character and I think a lot about how I come across to everyone I meet. I want them to have a good experience – even if they hate every opinion I have.

The waitress who served my date and me had a personal brand with me; and I had one with her. I like to think that she thought I was pleasant, and I certainly thought she was polite and excellent at her job (and tipped her accordingly). My date also had a personal brand with me and the waitress – we both thought he was rude.

The reality is, my date wasn't actually rude. He was just unaware. And therein lies the difference between those who take control of their reputation and those who do not. I made sure the waitress heard me when I said thank you and, in doing so, I was proactively shaping her impression of me as a person. My date was unconsciously shaping his reputation with her (and me), because he wasn't even thinking about it.

It's no longer *just about the people you meet in real life that forms your reputation*. It's not just one-to-one. Social media has enabled us to build what I call one-to-many relationships. I reach hundreds of thousands, sometimes millions of people per week. Building your personal brand, specifically online, allows you to grow your reputation, at scale.

Prior to social media, scaling your reputation was hard, if not impossible. I remember, when I was a recruiter, I was given the target of making 100 calls per day because they knew if recruiters hit that key performance indicator, at least a handful of those calls would turn into conversations and a few of those conversations would turn into business. The problem is, it's almost impossible to speak to anyone at length when you have that many calls to make each day, which means the number of meaningful relationships you build through those calls is a tiny proportion – I'm talking 3 out of 100. There is a finite amount of time in a day and so, using this approach, there is only a finite number of people you can connect with.

The beauty of growing your personal brand online is that the number of people you can reach in a day is almost infinite. If we start managing our reputations at scale – aka using social media to build our personal brands – we can reach one million people in 24 hours, instead of only being able to call 100 and reach about 4. This is all about getting people to know who you are in a way that is manageable but also incredibly scalable.

Back to basics: what is a personal brand?

One of the biggest mistakes many people make is hearing the word 'brand' and immediately thinking that their personal brand is something separate, and completely disassociated, from who they are. They think about traditional branding, where you invent a brand, typically for a business.

But here is the thing, you cannot invent your personal brand because it's based on, and intrinsically tied to, your personality. That's why the 'personal' bit is so important. This also means that, whether you have been intentional about building it or not, you already have a personal brand. The reason this first chapter is about reputation at scale is because that is the essence of what your personal brand allows you to do. It's a super-efficient and supercharged way of taking your personality and scaling it up – while also building the credibility and rapport you'd get from working on a one-on-one basis.

A lot of the blockers that you might have around building your personal brand are centred on ego, pride and being worried about what other people think of you. I was certainly in that place when I first started building mine. But the thing is, in almost all cases, you do not have those worries when you enter a one-to-one conversation. Most of us do not freak out when we are saying 'thank you' to the barista for serving us our coffee, or when we are bringing up a potentially challenging problem or topic at work or with friends. So, reframing personal branding as 'one-on-one interactions, but at scale', helps shift your mindset from 'what if they don't like me?' to 'I'll be fine if they don't'. And that is the basis of a strong personal brand – and of strong self-esteem.

Constructive interference

Attention. The single most valuable currency in 2024. Most of us understand that the more attention you get from the right people, the more opportunities you will receive. In a business that could mean sales, market share, investment. This is also true for your personal brand. When you start intentionally thinking about what you are doing, how you are behaving and what you are putting out into the world, you begin to reverse engineer what you want your outcome to be and align your actions to that. Aka, if you are clear on what you want, and who you need in your network to make that happen, you can tailor your content and actions to that outcome. I told you: personal branding is not an ego-driven activity, it's a strategic marketing imperative.

In physics, there's a law known as constructive interference. The principle is simple: when two frequencies of the same wavelength interact in such a way that they are aligned, they double in size.

As humans, the energy of our emotional state can be measured in a frequency. Research has found that the highest frequency emotion is authenticity, and not by a little, but by a lot: 400× more than love, actually.[1] When you have interactions with someone, whether it's face to face or online, there is an energy exchange that takes place. If you go into that interaction with authenticity, and the person you are engaging with is also emitting that same emotion, your frequency will double. And that is why authenticity is so damn powerful. It's authentic content that goes viral; it's why people can attract thousands to speaking engagements where they talk about their failures and their losses. Authenticity is the only thing powerful enough to make our frequency double its wavelength. This is not some woo-woo fluff – it's scientifically measured and proven.

If you put yourself out there authentically – if you take control and commit to being yourself and are completely OK with the consequences of being yourself – then scaling your personal brand will have an immeasurable impact on your life, compared to if you just toe the line and do what everyone else is doing. Why do you think I have so many followers? Or Steven Bartlett gets so many downloads of his podcast, 'Diary of the CEO', or Elon Musk is so famous and successful? Love us or hate us, we are all authentic.

Back to the science, this energy exchange happens whether you are consciously controlling it or not, so the first step is to take control of your personal brand and be aware of how you are behaving in every interaction you have with others – and making sure you are being authentic in those interactions. If you do not take control of your personal brand and aren't consciously thinking about it, then at the very best you will miss out on opportunities, and at worst people will think you are an a**hole.

And this is never more important than with first impressions. You have one-tenth of a second before someone makes an assumption about you. When you know who you are, are conscious of how you come across to other people, and are able and willing to take control of the first impressions they make of you, you are giving yourself the best shot of making that impression a positive one. And thus, inviting opportunity with open arms.

Being conscious of how you come across to others is absolutely essential. But, of course, your personal brand is about so much more than just how you look. There are four main components to your personal brand:

- How you look.

- How you act.

- What you know.

- What you believe.

Take a piece of paper and grab a pen. I want you to write down the four key points above, with some space underneath for you to fill in your blanks. Start with how you look, because that will be what people use to form their first impressions. What do you want people to think about you? Who do you want to be to them? Your outfit, hair, make-up (if you wear it), choices should reflect that.

From there you move to how you act – does the way you behave back up how you look? If you look like you have got your s**t together, will that come across in your actions? Second impressions can be even more important than first impressions. A good first impression might open the door of opportunity, but if you lack integrity or substance – or, most importantly, authenticity – that door will get slammed right in your face. The day someone meets me and says, 'Wow, you're so different to how you come across online', is the day I've failed.

Once you have nailed down how you are coming across, you want to think about the value you can add. What is the secret sauce that only you can share? Remember this is about what *you* know about your subject – your lived experience is the difference between what you offer and what someone could learn from Google. So many people do not build their personal brand because they tell themselves they are not an expert, or worse, there are other experts in their space already. The reality is, while you might be able to find information about personal branding from other people on Google, what you will not find is my story; *why* I believe what I believe, *how* I know what I know or *why* I am even writing this book. That is my knowledge, my story – and my competitive advantage.

Finally, I want you to think about what you believe in. What are your values? These are the things that will make people buy into you, your story and your knowledge over someone else. And some might not buy into you, which is a wonderful thing. That is why being authentic in your personal brand is so important, it attracts who you want it to attract and repels who you want it to repel. I personally believe intrinsically that self-belief, self-confidence and accountability are at the epicentre of success. If you can take accountability for your own life and stop waiting for someone to tell you what to do, you will be successful. And if you are reading this book right now, chances are, you are starting to think that too.

Accountability plays a role in all four of the elements of your personal brand. I've changed the way I dress because I want to be accountable for how people perceive me. I always say 'thank you' to the barista or my Uber driver because I want to be accountable for how I act and, therefore, reinforce people's first impression of me. I give 100% of my knowledge away for free online and in talks because I want to share what I've learned, and for people to think of me as an expert. Finally, authenticity and honesty are deeply tied into my content because I am confident enough to share the reality of my life, my values. It's a process of layering one thing on to the next until you find the way to present who you authentically are to the world in a way that other people will understand – and in a way that makes you feel understood.

You miss 100% of the shots you don't take.

—*Wayne Gretzky*

It's also important to realise that the more you can share about yourself and the more authentic you are with how you show up in the world and online, the more opportunities you have to make that positive impression on people. Wayne Gretzky has it right – you have to put yourself out there and try. That might lead to failure, but it might not. One thing I do know is that if you fail to take control of your personal brand and put your authentic self out there every chance you get, you will definitely miss out on opportunities.

Control your value

Here are two identical bottles of water (Figure 1.1). Tell me, what is the difference between the two, other than the price? They're both the same size, same contents (still), and both sold in the same country. Any ideas?

The only difference between these two water bottles is one is sold in a supermarket and the other at an airport. So, why is the price so different? Because there are limited options of where someone can purchase a bottle of water at an airport – despite being able to buy water on a plane, fill up a bottle at a tap or even get it free with your meal, there is the perception of scarcity and therefore its value increases.

When you take control of your personal brand, you are placing yourself at the airport rather than in a supermarket. You put yourself in the minority, not the majority and are therefore intentionally increasing your demand as an individual, and therefore your value. The result?

$0.99 $4.99

Figure 1.1: Two water bottles.

Being able to charge the metaphorical price of $4.99 vs. $0.99. And who wants to be a $0.99 bottle of water, anyway?

So, when you are focusing on consciously taking control of your personal brand, you are shaping yourself into someone who is an expert on a particular topic; someone who is confident talking about that topic and who is putting themselves out there as an expert in that topic – thus ensuring you are viewed as a $4.99 bottle of water, and not a $0.99 one. This is why you must be relentless in giving 100% of your knowledge away for free in your content, without asking for anything in return. Do not gatekeep. In sharing, you are saying, 'I'm great at this, and you can pay me or not, but I'm going to show you how great I am without asking for anything from you.'

And, look, I get it. Why should you give your knowledge away for free when you could get paid? Well, hear me out. When you give your knowledge away for free, people think you are credible. They trust you for advice and think you know what you are talking about. And, sure, your competitors might not share their knowledge because *they* charge for it. But copying them is an emotional and closed-mindset decision. Because the reality is, no one wants to be sold to but everyone wants to buy. When you share your knowledge and results for free, people convince themselves to buy from you without you having to ask them to, which makes you more valuable. And let's be honest, look at all the people with strong personal brands you follow – I bet 99% of them are teaching you something you are interested in learning or are advising on a problem you want solved. You trust them, and are therefore willing to give them the most valuable thing you own: your attention. Attention compounds into more attention – because 92% of people trust the opinion of strangers more vs. a company brand (their likes and comments equate to approval ratings online)[2] – and it's attention that builds a personal brand. It's also what will constantly and consistently increase your value.

Research by Gallup has found that 70% of our decisions are based on emotional factors.[3] This is also true when we are making buying decisions. Whether you are trying to attract B2B clients or consumers into your network – or even a hiring manager to help you get a new job – remember that these people base 70% of their decision on emotion. This is why being authentic in your personal branding content is so important; it helps you build relationships on an emotional level, *again* increasing your value. And I do not know about you, but it's pretty easy to break a contract, but it's pretty hard to break a relationship. Basically, the more authentically you share who you are in your personal brand and the more deeply people buy into you, the more you concrete people's desire to work with you, and only you. You're future-proofing your pipeline of career opportunities, clients, employees – and success.

This is no different to the fundamental premise that underpins all good marketing – good marketing does not sell a product or feature, it sells hopes, dreams, lifestyles and painkillers. No-one buys a drill because they want a drill; they buy a drill because they want a hole in a wall. It sells an outcome rather than the product itself.

With your personal brand, it's no different. Let's say you are a virtual assistant – there are thousands of people offering admin services right now. What you do not want to do is sell yourself as providing admin support. Instead, sell yourself as someone who gives busy executives more time to spend with their families or on their hobbies; or makes sure they never have to book an appointment or answer an email again. Share stories about how you gave a CEO back five hours per week, or how you helped them plan their anniversary surprise for their husband or wife.

When you give your knowledge away for free and when you share the outcomes you provide for clients, you can tap into the pain that you solve for your ideal audience and create resonance with them, which wins attention, gains credibility and will position you as *THE* choice, not just *A* choice among many. Heck, you'll be a $4.99 bottle of water by the time I'm done with you. But more on that in Chapter 5.

It's never too late to leave a legacy

I think a lot of people feel like they are late to the party with building their personal brand. Maybe you are one of those people. But it's never too late to take control of your reputation and become accountable for what you want your life to look like. If you came to this early in your career, congratulations – you have realised that your reputation is your ticket to getting ahead. If you are a senior executive who is thinking you wish you'd known sooner? Brilliant. In this book you are going to learn how to legacy plan your exit and guarantee opportunities when you eventually decide to move on, or even retire.

Unconvinced? Let's look at this another way – if you were overweight and unfit at 50, and a doctor told you to lose weight and get in shape otherwise you were likely to have a heart attack within the next couple of years, you'd change your diet and you'd get yourself to the gym, wouldn't you? You wouldn't tell yourself you'd left it too late and accept your fate. But even if you ignored your doctor's advice, you'd be making a choice. And I suppose that is all I'm asking you to do – make a conscious choice to control your personal brand and your reputation (and therefore life!), or continue unconsciously shaping other people's perceptions of you and leave your destiny up to them. I know which one I'd choose.

Getting Klowt: change your career, change your life

When I first started Klowt, we signed a handful of clients pretty quickly. One of those clients, Steve, came to us to help reinvent his reputation. He had a pretty colourful past, had been really successful quite young and had enjoyed all of the hard partying and bad decisions that came with that level of success. His reputation wasn't good. But, when he came to us, he'd been working hard on himself and was ready to enter the next stage of his life with a sensible, and credible, hat on. He was no longer the person those in his industry knew him to be - and our remit was to reshape his reputation and help him take control of what people thought of him, and his career in the process.

Within a few years, we helped Steve go from zero followers to having an audience of nearly 100,000 - people were sliding into his direct messages, asking to work with him every single month. Now, he's a consultant who charges upwards of $3,500 for a day's work. He moved into a bigger house, bought an amazing car, took his family on incredible trips - all because he focused on intentionally taking control of his reputation. Building his personal brand did not just change his career and transform his reputation; it transformed his life.

If you are thinking that it's too late in your career for you to change your reputation and refocus, let's just put something into perspective: Colonel Sanders was in his sixties when he founded KFC. Still unsure? The question you need to ask yourself, then, is, do you want to be a Van Gogh or a Picasso? While a brilliant artist, Van Gogh died penniless after taking his own life. Picasso, on the other hand, died with a fortune of millions and was well known and respected in his lifetime. While there were many differences between the two, from the outside it appears that a major contributor to Picasso's success is that he took control of his personal brand.

Picasso was sociable, networked and made sure people knew who he was and what he did. He made connections with other artists, writers, politicians and people in positions of power. Van Gogh, on the other hand, had a much smaller network. His primary connection to the art world was through his brother. He did not take control of his personal brand in his lifetime, much less scale it.

Self-promotion is not a dirty word. If you want to get ahead, you have to get comfortable with shouting about who you are, what you do and the talent you have. And I get it, that can feel, well, gross. Particularly for the Brits among you, we feel like it's a deadly sin to talk about our achievements. But let me tell you something: your legacy will be nothing but the impact that you have on this world, whether that's on ten people you have met personally in your life or on 100 million people whom you have impacted through your content and personal brand. Both Picasso and Van Gogh left a legacy and created something of value in this world, but Picasso got to make the most of that value whereas Van Gogh did not.

One thing I'll give Van Gogh credit for, though, is that you do not need validation to create something of value. When you are able to disconnect your sense of value from other people's validation of you, whether that's through likes on social media posts or comments on YouTube videos, you'll be in a very powerful position. And that goes far deeper than just the content you post online. When you can put your head above the parapet and let go of the need for validation from your friends, family, spouse, boss and strangers, you go from a place of constantly worrying about whether you are doing the wrong thing, to a place of 'I'll be OK, even if I do'. I am lucky enough to have reached this place with my own content – and my life. I do not treat social media, or my personal brand, like a source of validation for my personality, but rather a distribution channel for it. This book will help you get there too. No longer will you refresh your LinkedIn feed or Instagram story to see who has liked or engaged. Being able to disassociate your opinion of yourself from other people's opinion of you is an incredible gift to give yourself and the key to building a life that you love and have no regrets about.

Amelia's words to live by

These are my 'rules' for life. They'll help you build your personal brand, but they'll also help you live a happier, more confident life filled with opportunities you deserve.

1. **Just f**king post it**

    Nothing is that deep. The things you are worrying about happening probably will not happen. And even if they do, you'll be fine. Stop letting fear dictate your actions and just f**king post it.

2. **Afford to tell the truth**

    Be 100% OK with the consequences of being yourself. Your personality is a lot like a magnet. It attracts who you want it to attract and repels who you want it to repel. It's like a pre-built filter to ensure you are not wasting time and energy on people who do not deserve or want it. There is a real power to being disliked. If you aren't willing to be hated by people you do not like, you cannot expect to be loved by those you do.

3. **Do not take it personally**

If you know it's not true, why do you care? Someone says something mean, someone trolls you online, someone disagrees with your opinion. . . I get trolled all the time for how I look, what I say, who I am. I get told I'm ugly, I'm stupid, I have no credibility – none of it is true, so why would I get upset about it? I have to caveat this with, I post about 150 pieces of content a month, and this rarely happens. But when it does, I genuinely do not care – in life and online – because why are you accepting someone's poor opinion of you over your own opinion of yourself? We cannot trust other people's opinions and thought processes about us more than we trust our own opinions about ourselves. You're the main character in your story, so stop giving screen time to shoddy support acts.

4. **Done well is better than perfect**

Do not overthink your content. You can spend hours trying to write the perfect post (I know, I fell into this trap when I started) only to share it and have 70 people see it before it's replaced in the feed by something else. What a waste of time! There's no such thing as perfect, so write it and then refer to rule #1!

5. **Your message is so much more important than your medium**

It can be easy to get hung up on making sure that none of your content contains typos, but your message is more important than that. Look at Steven Bartlett. I've seen tons of his content going out with spelling mistakes in it and no one thinks he's an idiot – we all buy his books, listen to his podcast and read his content because we trust and value his message more than his medium. Sure, a spelling mistake is not ideal, and I'd advocate investing in Grammarly but, in all honesty, do not sweat it if something is not perfect. It makes you human, which is what makes your content so endearing.

I recently had someone message me asking if I knew of any apps that would filter her face in video content. My response was, 'Why would you want to filter your face?' I understand that you might be scared of putting yourself out there online, but how much worse would it be if someone met you and did not recognise you in real life? That's not authentic. You have to afford to be yourself and be completely OK with the consequences of doing so.

I post a weekly vlog on YouTube, often with no make-up, walking around my house in a pair of old tracksuit bottoms, sharing my thoughts and my life. Could I do my hair and make-up perfectly every time? Maybe. Would I want to? No. I am intentional about what I share, sure. I want to make sure I am crafting a perception of who I am, but that perception needs to remain human and real, and the reality of my life is often that I am in a tracksuit with no make-up on – as are other people, which helps us form a connection. Why would I want to filter that?

None of your content will ever be perfect, and you will never look perfect, so stop trying to compete in that race. No one has ever contacted me and said, 'I loved your message but wish you'd put more make-up on'. The reality is, the more you filter yourself, the more you water yourself down and therefore the less you stand out. That is the opposite of what you want to achieve. The whole point of any personal brand is to stand out.

At the beginning of this chapter I told you about constructive interference and how authenticity is the highest frequency of energy you can emit as a person. I told you that when two wavelengths on the same frequency meet, they double. If you can be OK with being completely authentic and putting yourself out there, you will act as a magnet to attract other authentic, genuine people into your life. That's where the opportunity lies, and isn't that a wonderful thing? Stick a camera in your face and get to work!

Click moments

Personal branding is all about taking control. And trust me when I tell you, you have way more control over your life than you realise. Taking control of our personal brands is an important stepping stone to taking complete control of your life. But we need to ensure we do not get in our own way, so remember my five rules:

1. Just f**ing post it.

2. Afford to tell the truth.

3. Do not take it personally.

4. There is no such thing as a perfect piece of content.

5. Your message is so much more important than your medium.

Oh, and make sure they spell your name right.

2

Defining your why

When you're aligned with your personal brand strategy, everything just seems to flow. When I'm on fire, I'm excited to share what I'm doing, inspiration comes naturally and everything feels like it's aligned. That excitement radiates through what I am posting and it naturally draws people, and opportunities, in. When I'm in this space, my posts go viral. Now, I am not saying that is the point of this (dream bigger than 10k likes, people!) but you get my drift. When I am being true to myself and authentically sharing who that person is, I get attention, inbound leads, PR opportunities, podcast invites and speaking gigs. I've even landed TV opportunities.

When your personal brand is working for you, it's as though you're in the centre of a golden circle and every opportunity you've ever wished for (but didn't know how to get) is landing in your lap. Sometimes you get given opportunities you didn't even realise you wanted. It feels amazing, and it all comes from the excitable, authentic energy you're putting out into the world. Remember what I said about constructive interference and authenticity being 4000× more powerful than love? It's that, but in action.

When everything feels as though it's flowing, that's a great sign that you've taken control of your personal brand. That's not to say that it's easy – it takes work – but when what you're doing is in alignment with your 'why', it feels almost effortless. You won't be worrying about your results because they'll just happen. You won't get writer's block. You will attract the right people. People will start referring business to you, or tagging you in comments on other people's posts, presenting you with incredible opportunities.

And the more you can focus on what you're excited and passionate about, the more you can expand that golden circle, and bring more people and opportunities within it for yourself. So, how do you create that golden circle for yourself?

Get clear on your goals

Why are you doing this? No, seriously, answer the question. Why do you want to build your personal brand? Knowing the goal is the first step to helping you build a strong one. I want to be very clear – your goal should not be to get more likes or followers. Likes, while great key performance indicators (KPIs), are not going to pay your bills, or facilitate opportunities. And, on a personal level, they're definitely not going to make you feel loved or special, and they won't help you develop your knowledge. Chasing likes is a dangerous game and can often lead you to a negative place that isn't beneficial to anyone, let alone you.

I know this only too well. When I was younger, I had a pretty bad eating disorder. And part of the cycle that perpetuated that eating disorder, for me, was my use of social media. I would post a picture of myself online having lost a few kilos and, to be honest, looking really skinny. I'd get comments like, 'You look so amazing!' This perpetuated the idea that, if I didn't continue to look that way and seek validation from strangers, I was in some way not good enough. I'm not saying this was the cause of my eating disorder, but it certainly perpetuated it.

One of the things I say, most frequently, to my clients is, 'So, dream bigger than 10,000 likes'. (I've even said it to you once already!) Because what you're doing is about so much more than your social media following – it's about your personal growth, and self-worth. You have to aim for more than just superficial engagement. Sure, you need attention, but it has to be the right attention – you need people to see you to get the opportunities you deserve, but you don't need everyone to like you. Gosh, *you* don't even like everyone!

As I write this book, I am getting, and have had, many amazing opportunities, but if I'm honest? The greatest achievement I have had off the back of building my personal brand is my confidence. I have self-esteem by the truckload. And, trust me, I know how easy it is to post something, get five likes and then want to delete it because 'no one liked it', but let me reframe this for you. If five people came up to you right now and said, 'Wow, I think you're awesome, I want to know more about you!', would you feel disappointed, or excited? When you can let go of fixating on vanity metrics and instead focus on your goals, amazing things happen. So, dream bigger than 10,000 likes.

And, look, I get it, you might think that's easy for me to say as someone with 250,000 followers on social media, but do you know how I got there? By not caring *how many* people follow me, and by caring *who* was following me and whether or not what I was sharing was valuable to them and authentic to me.

When you first start out, I know it can be hard to come at growing your personal brand from that place. Because, certainly initially, the likes, followers and shares are the metrics that show you whether your personal brand activities are being successful online, but I promise you, the more content you post, the less you'll care about the numbers and the more confident you'll be in being 100% authentically yourself.

Think of this a little bit like dating. When you are dating, especially when you're younger, you probably spent at least the first two or three dates with someone new worrying about whether they like you. It's only once you begin to feel more comfortable with them that you start to consider whether *you like them*. It's very easy to make dating all about the other person, and to forget about yourself. Personal branding is very similar because you often make it all about whether other people like what you have to say and the reality is, it's all about whether *you* like what you have to say.

Building your confidence is a really important part of your personal brand journey, and what I can tell you is that the sooner you can reach the point where you are confident in yourself (and stop caring about what other people think of you and your opinions), the better. It took me four, maybe, five years to get to this point, but I've distilled the knowledge I've gained in that time into this book, so you'll get there much faster than me.

Differentiating your 'why' from your goals

There's a difference between your 'why' and your goals. My 'why' (vision) is to inspire people to be 100% comfortable with the consequences of being themselves, to love the skin they're in and reach their potential with the confidence that it will all work out. My goal (mission) is to help 1 million people to build their personal brand. Another one of my goals is to be financially free; to be able to pick my kids up from school and not worry about work and to be able to travel the world with the people I love. The KPIs surrounding my goal are therefore centred around reach, audience profile, the stages I'm on, the podcasts I guest feature on, the people I interview, the events I attend. All are strategic actions I am taking to align to my overall goal, which ultimately enables my 'why'. The 'why' is *why* I am doing what I do. The goal is what I need to make happen.

This wasn't how I started, though. If you'd asked me for my 'why' back when I first began posting content on LinkedIn, I'd have told you it was to convince my then-CEO that building personal brands was the gateway to generating inbound business. I'd worked out that people really did buy from people, and most of our business came from individuals within the organisation. And so, my goal was focused on how I could get as many likes and as much engagement as possible on my content, in as short a time as possible.

When I was headhunted and moved to 11 Investments, my 'why' became helping attract more employees and business through personal branding. My 'why' evolved yet again when I left to set up Klowt. My 'why' then was to get paid doing something I love. I have evolved a fair bit since then, as have my 'why' and my goals.

What I've come to realise throughout this process, is that all of those 'whys', from proving my then-CEO wrong, to building a reputation as a thought leader, to generating leads for my own business were in fact goals, not a deeper 'why'. My big 'whys' are exactly what I shared with you at the start of this section and are intrinsically linked to the life I want to live.

But I only figured these big whys out about 18 months before writing this book, by which time I had been actively focusing on my personal brand for five years – so while I'm sharing a process to help you uncover your 'why', know that it could well take some time before you truly understand your deeper purpose. And that's OK.

All the incremental goals I've had along the way, even those that I mistakenly believed were my 'why', have acted as stepping stones to bring me closer and closer to living a meaningful life. I know that answering the question, 'what is my "why"?' is a hard one. It's a lot like when someone asks who you are, or what your values are. It can be hard to articulate. It's also not something I am qualified to help you answer.

I am not your life coach. But what I will tell you is you'll know when you've found it. And that is what will happen, when you stop searching and just align your actions to the things that make you feel most fulfilled and good – things just begin to flow. And when things flow, the purpose and meaning of your life will flow right into your lap, often when you least expect it.

And that is what makes me so excited in writing this book. I know how amazing it feels when you get to a point where everything just aligns. I love my life, and I have moments of thinking, *wow, I am living the life I've always wanted*. I want you to feel that way too. But you won't get there unless you start taking action and laying the foundations of what you want your personal brand – and life to look like.

The other reason it's so important to get clear on your 'why' is because this is what will catch you when motivation doesn't. None of us are motivated seven days a week, 365 days a year, but your 'why' can give you the push to keep creating and sharing content, even on days when it's the last thing you want to do. Being clear about *why* you are taking control of your personal brand, and what you want to achieve by doing so, will help you maintain discipline. Building your personal brand is 10% content, 90% consistency in posting it.

Besides, your 'why' will ultimately lead to your core messaging. When you know *why* you're doing what you're doing, it's much easier to identify what you really believe in and therefore what topics you should be talking about.

Exercise: writing your mission statement

Your mission statement should encapsulate your big 'why' and also set out your core goal (or goals). The following process will help you uncover your 'why' and put that into a simple, tangible statement that you can refer back to again and again.

To give you a kick start, I'm on a mission *to inspire one million people to build their personal brand, reach their potential and attract every single opportunity they deserve.* The way I can do that is by growing my own personal brand to put myself in front of more people and inspire them to do the same – like with this book.

One piece of advice before you dive into this exercise: the more specific you can be, the better. When you set yourself a mission, and then identify the goals that will act as the stepping stones to get you there, be specific at every stage, because the more targeted you can be, the more likely you are to achieve not only your individual goals but your bigger mission, your 'why'. Look at my mission, it's not just to help people build their personal brand, it's to help *one million people* build their personal brand. Or think of the difference in approach if your goal was to get a job as a marketing manager, versus a job as senior marketing manager at Nike. Get it? Right, let's get to work.

What do you value most? What is most important to you?

When I say values, I mean the things that are non-negotiable in your life. I don't mean single words like 'family' or 'trust'. I want you to dig into how those words show up in your life. It can be helpful to reframe the question to be, 'What needs to happen to feel like you're doing a good job?' or ask yourself, 'What do my friends value in me?'

For example, rather than writing 'family', you might write, 'I really care about my wife thinking I'm a good person and her being proud of me'.

These values can also evolve and grow as you do, so what you write down now might change in a year or in five years' time. Take some time now to write down your five non-negotiables that you would like to have in your life that show you that you're enjoying it as much as possible.

What are you most passionate about?

The next thing I want you to do is write down five things that you're passionate about. If you're not sure how to answer that, what brings you joy? These don't have to be work-related. They can be anything that brings you joy and makes you feel fulfilled. It might be gardening, playing games with your kids, even the football club you support. Again, take some time to think about and write down the five things you're most passionate about.

What are your most significant professional and personal goals? What does the best version of you look like?

Look back over your career so far and then think about where you want your career to go. Let's say your values are that you want to be home for bed and bath time with your kids every night and you want your wife to be proud of you. Your passions are Arsenal football club and taking your family on a beach holiday every year. Your skills are sales and closing really big deals.

When you look at your career trajectory, you can see that you have gone from an entry-level sales position to being the sales director. However, because a lot of your calls are in America, you can't clock-off at 5 p.m. every day, which means you're not meeting your non-negotiables, are you? To live the life you aspire to have, and to meet all the things you've just told me are very important, perhaps you need to change your job. Or become a consultant. Would working as a fractional Sales Director help you better align with your 'why'?

Becoming a consultant would give you more control over your time, allowing you to get home for your kids each day. You could earn more money as a consultant, which will give you the financial freedom to pay for the family holidays you want to go on. All of a sudden, your 'why' has shifted from wanting to generate new business for your current role, to going self-employed – and completely changing your life.

What does the best version of you look like in terms of your career, relationships and achievements? Make a note of those goals here.

What do other people consider to be your greatest strengths?

Now, it's time to look at your strengths. What do your friends, family and colleagues consider your greatest strengths? The reason I ask what your loved ones think your strengths are, is because it can be hard to identify them yourself. We're all so self-critical, sometimes the thing you're great at is the thing you think you need to improve the most. Asking people in your life for this kind of feedback is actually really insightful, and super powerful. Once you've identified those strengths, you've got a framework to how you're going to grow your personal brand.

An example: if one of my friends said I was really articulate and great at inspiring people, that might lead me to public speaking as a 'how' for growing my personal brand. But if I was more introverted, video content or public speaking might be my worst nightmare – and potentially something I wasn't very good at. However, my writing might be really strong so instead I could look at how to leverage that by writing articles or even books. You get where I am going with this?

When it comes to building your personal branding, too many people push themselves outside of their comfort zone by producing video content, for instance, even though they are, quite frankly, bad at it – all because someone has told them they should. But putting out something you're not good at isn't going to help promote yourself, is it? That's not to say you shouldn't try video – I sucked at it for months before I realised how to deliver a message with impact – but understanding your strengths means you can play to them, which will make getting out of the gates with your personal brand a heck of a lot easier.

Take a moment now to write down what your friends, colleagues and loved ones would consider your top three to five strengths.

What legacy do you want to leave behind? How can your skills help you do that?

I've been building my personal brand for some time now, and in my experience most people start to post content and build their brand because someone told them they should. Perhaps that's why you're reading this book. I certainly didn't start developing my personal brand with legacy in mind. However, the more I posted content, the more speaking gigs I did and the more direct messages I'd received from people telling me they were inspired to do the same, the more obvious the legacy side of taking control of my personal brand became.

When I say legacy, I don't mean what you'll leave behind when you die – I mean what do you want to be known for? What do you want people to say about you when you're not in the room? How do you want people to introduce you to others? So, my legacy – or my end goal, to frame it a different way – is for people to say, 'That woman changed my life' after they've seen me speaking on stage. I want them to have the confidence to build their brand and take control of their, well, life.

As I said at the start of this book, you don't really build your personal brand, you take control of it. You have a personal brand already, whether you like it or not, but if you don't take control of it, you might not like what it – and your legacy – look like.

I've also asked you what skills you have that can help you get there, 'there' being your legacy, because it's going to be difficult to achieve your goals without understanding what you're leveraging to get there. Skills might encompass some of the strengths you identified earlier, or they might be expertise or a practical skill that you possess.

Think back to the example of the water bottles I shared in Chapter 1. This step in the process of finding your why and writing your mission statement is about focusing on what is unique *to you* and how you can use your unique combination of knowledge, strengths, skills and expertise to position yourself as the bottle of water at the airport that's worth $4.99, rather than the bottle in the supermarket that's worth $0.99.

One skill alone won't make you unique, but your stack of skills will, and the sooner you can identify those, the sooner you can position yourself as unique: *the* choice, not just *a* choice among many, making you very valuable indeed.

[blank box]

Write your mission statement

Now that you've answered all of those questions you're ready to write your mission statement, which follows a very simple format:

I will [action] by [skills] to [desired result or outcome].

For example, I will create an inspiring podcast, for people interested in psychology, to help them apply science-based learning to transform their lives with everyday habits and actions.

[blank box]

When you read your mission statement back, you should feel excited by it. And if you don't, you did it wrong. My mission statement in its entirety is *to inspire one million people to build their personal brand, reach their potential and attract every single opportunity they deserve.* I hope in many ways I am achieving that with this book – but don't write something because it sounds like mine. It should be unique, personal and feel really motivating. Write something that, when you read it back, makes you think Hell, yeah! That's me! This mission statement is what will get you out of bed each and every day and it will help you create and share content that not only excites you, but that excites many other people too.

This mission statement will sit at the very top of your personal branding pyramid, and everything else that follows comes beneath it. Now that you know your mission statement and have connected to your why, it's time to take some action.

Get out of your own way

One of the reasons I've suggested you ask your colleagues, friends and family to tell you what they think your biggest strengths are, is because of the confidence that will give you. The first steps to building your personal brand are often the hardest. The number one reason why people never take control of their personal brand or reputation is because of fear their friends will screenshot their content and judge them – or worse, share it in the WhatsApp chat and laugh.

You're smiling as you read that now, because you know it's true! Every time I say this to one of my clients, they laugh, because we *all* have this reaction to the idea of putting ourselves out there. We worry that other people are going to make fun of us, but the reality is that those people don't matter – they also don't care anywhere near as much as we think they do. And besides, even if they do laugh at you for the first few months you're posting, it won't be long before they ask you how you did it. My friends thought I was weird for posting content on LinkedIn, now they attend my speaking gigs and ask for advice on how they can build theirs. First they call you crazy, then they ask you how you did it.

I remember there were a handful of friends who'd say things like 'Oh, you're getting a bit big for your boots. . .' Honestly, it stung a bit at the time, but I continued. I was so invested in building a better life for myself, I didn't have too much time to be worried about what passing comments people were making to my face and behind my back. Now, five years down the road, I'm running a successful business, I own my own home, I have a job I love – I've found my purpose in life and am, quite honestly, ahead of a lot of those people. Not just in my career, but in my life. Now they look at me and tell me that I'm really inspiring. I don't see them much any more. My real friends have been supportive since the day I hit 'post', whether they understood what I was doing or not. I have also met some incredible social media friends who have gone on to become some of my closest mates. (Another wonderful by-product of personal branding!) My point is, you might take some flak for walking down a path less trodden to start with, but usually, when people make fun of you or say 'you can't', they usually mean 'I can't'.

Click moments

Knowing your why will accelerate what you're able to achieve by taking control of your personal brand. It took me years to reach a truly aligned, purpose-driven 'why'. I'm not saying that you'll find yours by completing the exercise in this chapter (if you did, congrats!) but at least you're now thinking about what your deeper 'why' and purpose might be, which means you're way ahead of most other people.

Now you've got your 'why', it's time to use it to create your brand strategy.

3

What is a good brand strategy?

Everyone is talking about personal branding. That's likely the reason you're reading this book. But so few people actually do personal branding *well*. There are even creators and freelancers, pumping out advice, courses and paid subscriptions for how to build your brand online, without any real following of their own. The thing that most people lack when beginning their personal branding journey is a good strategy. Without that, you're screwed.

So, what does a good strategy look like? Well, a good brand strategy is comprised of four things:

- Goal.

- Audience.

- Content.

- Distribution and engagement.

Whenever I start working with a client, the first thing I do is ask them what their goal is. Beyond the leads, the influence, the followers, what are the hopes and ambitions that they have for their career? It might be an exit of their business, it might be they want to climb the corporate ladder and get the C-level job of their dreams, it might be as simple as 'freedom'. Whatever your goal is, it's important you know what it is, because without it, we can't work out what audience you need to attract in order to make the goal happen. And if we don't know who we are trying to attract, then how do we know what to talk about online? A good personal branding strategy starts with a defined goal.

This is where you and I are going to start, too. And, by the way, this personal branding stuff is about so much more than just the content you're putting out on social media. It's also about how you show up in meetings (are you always late with a Pret in hand or early with notes?) or the emails you're sending to your team (no one wants to be known as 'that person who always complains about the coffee machine being broken'). The strategy we set out now will transcend into the rest of your life, too. In the way you communicate who you are, period – whether that's to your 5,000 followers on Instagram or to the junior HR managers in the office kitchen. Your reputation matters, both on and offline, so should your strategy to shape it.

Reverse-engineering your strategy

One of the reasons I start with your goal when I'm helping build a personal branding strategy, is every tactic you need to deploy can be reverse-engineered from there. One of the goals that *I* want to achieve is to become financially free. I want to have active and passive income that match each other. If I get that, it'll help me achieve some of my 'whys'. Upping my income without increasing my workload would mean I could take my kids to school on time, and finish early on a Thursday so I can pick them up at 3.30 p.m. and spend the afternoon in the park with them. Or I could take a month off work and travel and not have to worry about paying the mortgage or running out of cash. Sounds dreamy.

Creating a personal brand strategy to achieve this goal means thinking: what do I actually need to do to become financially free? Well, first off, I need to earn some money and the best place to start there is an active income. The way I can generate that active income is by selling services, such as paid speaking. I need people to know that I offer paid speaking services though, so I'll put 'speaker' in my headline title on LinkedIn so that anyone who finds me there can see that I offer that.

I will probably also need to find some evidence of my previous work, so I'll start recording the speaking gigs I do and then cut them up into micro-content. I would plan to pitch myself onto other people's podcasts and talk about personal branding and mention the speaking gigs I do and why I do them. I would then want to post the micro-content I've taken from the speaking gigs and the podcasts and share them all over social media for the world to see that I, Amelia Sordell, am a speaker. All of these activities encourage people to think of me when they're looking for a speaker at an event in my niche. I've reverse-engineered a route to increasing my active income, and therefore financial freedom for myself.

It's starting with your goal, working out who you need to attract, and then targeting your activities, content topics and distribution around those people so they come into your network and make achieving your goal possible.

Another way to look at this goal-to-tactics route is this; I need to bring in more clients for my agency, Klowt, so that I can generate more revenue and pay myself a better salary. Now, who do I need to attract in order to win more revenue? Well, most of Klowt's ideal clients are C-suite level executives in a FTSE or Fortune organisations, or founders of scale-ups and small and medium-sized enterprises (SMEs). These are the people who need to attract amazing talent, win brand awareness and who need help to position themselves as an employer of choice. I can help them through personal branding. This is the first audience I need to attract in order to achieve my goal of more revenue, and therefore a better salary.

So how do I cut through the noise and reach these busy executives and founders? How can you work out what to say that is going to make them stop the scroll and pay attention to you and your content? Well, it starts with them – not you. One of the reasons I have managed to build a successful business selling personal branding services is not because I just talk about personal branding – which I do consistently – it's because I talk about things that my ideal audience will relate to.

My ideal audience are founders and busy executives, many of them working parents. I am also a founder, executive and working parent and so a lot of the content I share is talking about the challenges, successes, frustrations and musings of being a founder, executive and working parent. It creates resonance. It's human. And it appeals to the one thing that people find it very difficult to argue against – themselves.

But just posting things that resonate with your audience sometimes isn't enough. Almost all of my business comes directly from a contact point that the founder or executive has had with me, but sometimes it's not directly from me. Sometimes these people aren't even online, least of all looking for someone to build their personal brands, so if I only focus on them, I might find it hard to get the followers, impressions and reach I need to attract the leads I want. So, on top of sharing content that resonates with founders and executives, I also need to appeal to a secondary audience. I call these 'the ring of influence'. These are the people close to the executives and founders, like admin, assistants, marketing and sales teams. They're not quite who we're looking for, but they're close enough to gain us access to our ideal customer.

So, I begin to post a lot of content around helping *them* build a personal brand, and how it benefits their career and businesses as a whole. Then, when the topic of brand awareness, or, personal branding, thought leadership, or even increasing the sales pipeline of a business is brought up, guess whose name is likely to be mentioned? Mine.

We signed a client to Klowt recently who'd been talking to his executive assistant (EA) about personal branding and finding an agency to help. That evening his EA saw a post of mine on TikTok. She forwarded it to him and he signed a $100,000 contract with us a few weeks (and a handful of pitch meetings) later. At this point, I'd like to shout-out all of the executive assistants out there – I couldn't live without Amy, who is mine – it's a hard and thankless job and probably one of the most valuable in a business.

Always remember, even in the business-to-business (B2B) space, it's a *human being* who is making the buying decision. And human beings are often influenced by the people they trust most. Leverage that trust for a competitive advantage.

The ring of influence is how advertising has worked for decades. Just look at McDonald's. They market a tiny version of their meal to children, pop it in a special box with a limited edition toy, and call it a 'Happy Meal'. You can't build a multi-billion dollar business on a children's meal alone, but McDonald's knows that if they influence the children, they influence the parents. (If a kid is screaming that it's *so unfair* that all their friends get to go for Happy Meals on Fridays, even the most stern and nutritionally focused parents cave in!) And once those parents walk through the Golden Arches, they're almost always going to buy themselves some nuggets or a milkshake as a little treat on top of that $3.99 kids meal. Make sense?

The influencer effect

As I mentioned earlier, I cut my teeth in sales as a recruiter. And, as anyone who has done that job will know, it's brutal. It was almost impossible to hit target because our target was making 100 calls a day – eight hours on the phone! That's because when you're building one-to-one relationships it takes time. I mean, we've all online dated, right! And that is why social media is so powerful. Instead of spending 8 hours every single day trying to forge 100 relationships, you could spend 30 minutes creating some amazing content to reach 100,000. Instead of one-to-one, it's one-to-many.

When you take the one-to-many approach, you're able to chat with pretty much an infinite number of people all over the world – it's scalable. Calling people, or meeting people is not. There is a finite number of people you can speak to in 24 hours.

You can also get creative with how you create this influencer effect. Take PayPal's referrer scheme. It was a major success when it first launched and still continues to this day. PayPal offers a $10 payment to anyone who refers a friend to its platform, and the person who signs up also receives $10. You get the cash if the new user spends $5 on the platform within their first 30 days. What a great way to influence people, and turn customers into influencers working on your behalf!

PayPal is attaching a monetary value to its influence, but value doesn't need to have a financial figure attached. Take my content that's targeted at the 'ring of influence' around founders and executives, such as executive assistants – I'm adding value by sharing useful information that helps them to take control of and grow their personal brands. They become my referrers, because when the executive they work for needs some support changing public perception of them or becoming the go-to voice in their field on LinkedIn, I'm the person they think of.

I can't even tell you the number of people who have contacted me about working with Klowt, and who have started their message by telling me their assistant has been following me for years. Think about that when you come up with *your* personal brand strategy. Yes, you want to work out who you're targeting, but it's also a good idea to know how to reach their 'ring of influence' too.

Content is king

There are a few essential elements of good personal branding content. For a start, your content needs to be agile. You've got to be able to adapt – at speed – to changes in your industry and demonstrate to your followers that you're a front runner who's going to help them keep up. Make your content plan flexible enough that if huge news breaks, you're not scrambling around to make space for a post reacting to it, but consistent enough that you always have something to say. It also means that you have a plan in place for when life gets in the way.

I think people think I'm a content machine. I mean, I do post about 150 pieces of content per month, which is a lot. And I'm able to do that because I have a system in place to execute that volume. More on that later. And while I do have a pretty well-oiled content machine going, the reality is that I still have a life, and it often gets in the way of being able to maintain consistency online. Which makes it even more important for you to make the most of the times when you're inspired, creating as many content ideas as you can, so that for the days when you're feeling. . . not quite so sharp, you're covered.

And, by the way, there will be days, weeks, months when you're uninspired. Sometimes I sit at my computer and just stare, praying the words come. They often don't. When this happens – which it does often for me – just repurpose a piece of content that previously did well. I repost, remix, reuse as much old content as humanly possible. Aka, copy and paste something that performed well 6, 8, 12 months ago and post it again. Chances are, if it wasn't time-sensitive and it did well then, it will do well now.

That's a handy thing about social media – it moves so fast, content is quickly forgotten (also why you need to be consistent in posting it!). If you've done something before that worked, do it again. No one will notice. I've posted a single post a total of seven times to date and have yet to have anyone say, 'Er... didn't you post this before?' You don't need to reinvent the wheel. And the more content you share, the easier this becomes. I'll talk more about what this looks like later in the book.

It is also important to constantly iterate your content: don't be afraid to test new ideas, see what your followers are loving to engage with and then use their reactions as feedback to tweak your approach and improve the content you're sharing. We live in a rapidly changing world. By the time this book comes out, social media algorithms will have changed several times over and hundreds of different trends will have taken over TikTok and Instagram. What you're doing right now might not work in six months' time. And that is why you've got to completely remove your ego from your personal brand. You have to be unemotional about testing and learning and adapting to new platforms, new algorithms and new styles of sharing your message.

For example, last year I was smashing it with my video content. For months, every post I put out received more than 1,000 likes from exactly the right people I was trying to reach. Then the LinkedIn algorithm got an update, and all of a sudden, my engagement fell through the floor. I could have given up – and blamed the algorithm. Or, I could just change my approach and go again. Algorithms come and go, social media comes and goes – your reputation and your personal brand will live forever. So be headstrong in your messaging, but be flexible and adaptable in your approach.

Iteration is a natural part of life, especially in business. Just look at how mobile phones have evolved from being handheld bricks that allowed you to make calls and send text messages (and maybe play Snake, remember that?), to the smartphones we now have, which, by the way, give you more access to knowledge and power than Clinton had in the White House. Crazy! Everything from a journal, to a calculator, to a measuring tool and a camera are all neatly stored away in those little devices. Just goes to show what time does to technology – and to brands. Which also means you have absolutely no excuse not to open up your phone right now and share a quick LinkedIn Post or Instagram Reel.

Seek friends, not followers

Once you've decided who your audience is. It's time to talk top tactics when it comes to actually speaking to them. The best one I can give you? Build an audience of friends, not followers. Many people mistake racking up numbers on social media for a tactic that can grow your personal brand, but while having 30 million followers on TikTok might look impressive, it doesn't necessarily help your personal brand.

If you've gained loads of followers quickly, it's probably because your focus has been giving people a dopamine hit rather than building a relationship. You've shown them stuff they like (cats, food, cars. . .), not started a conversation that's actually worth having. And while that kind of content might get people to tap the 'like' button, it doesn't create any emotional connection with the person who's posted the content.

How many times have you been telling someone about a post you saw on TikTok or Instagram, but can't remember who posted it? (Me, daily.) It's because you have no connection with the creator of that content. The person behind that feed has only posted things to make you like *their content*, rather than posting things to make you like *them*. You're a follower, not a friend. You want to do the opposite of that with your personal brand.

Creating a loyal group of friends with your content is a bit like demonstrating to a date that you *really are* looking for something serious (I know, scary): you need to show you're actually invested in building a personal relationship with your audience. To do that, you need to give them something of yourself and show some vulnerability. Your content should give other people a window into who you are as a person, which means they get to know and like *you*, as well as liking your content. This creates a human connection. They feel like you're their mate, not just an influencer!

The method for doing this is pretty simple – instead of posting clickbait content, talk about things you're passionate about and that you're confident speaking about. Think about what content you can share that will help people get to know and like you as a person (no one likes a robot!). This is so important as you take more control of your personal brand, because you cannot build a successful personal brand by just getting loads of followers. You need people to develop a connection with you, and your content has to give them a reason to want to do that.

Getting Klowt: time to get personal

I was speaking at an event recently. When it was time for questions, a man in the audience put his hand up and asked me how he could make money from his TikTok account. It had 250,000 followers, he told me, and he'd built that following by posting Harry Potter film clips. People love them. He gets loads of likes. Millions in fact. That should be the perfect starting point for making money, right? Well, no, actually.

The problem here is he has a lot of followers, which is great. But he doesn't have any influence on those followers, because the only reason they follow him is because they love Harry Potter, not because they love him. I told him that he won't be able to monetise those followers unless he stops solely posting snippets of the movies and introduces himself.

I told him to inject himself into the content he's making, maybe start critiquing the movie scenes he shares, or revealing his take on the actions of the characters or the deeper meaning behind some of the stories in the books and films. . . People won't be prepared to pay money to just another guy who likes Harry Potter – they need to know who he is. When they have that personal connection, he'll be able to monetise his content, because he'll finally have influence. Essentially, this creator had built a significant following, but he hadn't built a personal brand.

Just be yourself

OK, I know what you're thinking. 'Just be yourself' is crap advice. And generally, I agree with you. Because who even are you? I'm still figuring that out myself. But, you do need to inject some personality into your content, add a touch of vulnerability and be OK with people thinking you're not the best thing since sliced bread. It will feel uncomfortable, probably a bit scary and whether you care to admit it or not, you will care what other people think, but it's so important that you really bring who you are to your personal brand online and offline. If people don't connect with you as a person, how can you expect them to be influenced by what you're saying?

When you think about it, the whole point of personal branding is to use your smart, wonderful, engaging self to build a reputation that is going to deliver you opportunities right into your inbox. You can't do that if you're copying and pasting other people's content and only following algorithmic hacks some personal branding 'guru' told you to use. You need to be more strategic. And that means it will take a little more effort on your part to be yourself. . . and longer to build a community of friends – but the extra time you put into being authentic with your content will pay the most incredible return on investment (ROI). Just ask Elon Musk's accountant.

So have a think about topics, experiences and lessons that feel authentic to you – and will resonate with your audience. It's why I talk so much about my screw-ups, because making mistakes is one thing that *all* of us have in common. I know that if I talk openly and honestly about when I've messed up, people will relate to me. Dare I say it, they like me. My imperfect stories might even help them feel more confident about overcoming their own challenges. This creates followers and friendships, which is why I have a circle of people who advocate for me and refer business to me – even if we've never met in real life.

The heart of your personal brand

If you've made it this far, you're serious about building a personal brand. Congratulations, you're better than 99% of people who know they should build their personal brand, but never take any action to do it. But we've not covered an essential part of this entire thing; what do you actually want to be *known* for? This should be at the heart of your strategy. It's the one thing that should NEVER change. You might want to be known for being an expert in leadership, or entrepreneurship. I want people to know me for personal branding. What is the one thing you want to be famous for? Because if you want to be famous, you have to be famous for *something*.

That is not to say you can't talk about other things. We've already discussed how I leverage my own f**k-ups and mistakes to attract other founders and executives who've made the same ones, but personal branding is always at the heart of my strategy, because that is what I need to be known for to make my goals happen. And that is why it's so important to be razor clear on what that thing is. You can't flip-flop between marketing one day, sales the next, politics on Wednesday and back to marketing next Tuesday. You'll confuse your audience, you'll confuse yourself and you'll give people no reason to follow you consistently, because you're not even consistent. So, what do you want to be known for?

Top tip for ensuring your personal brand is consistent on social media; make sure that your message is the same, but that you contextualise it for the platform you're sharing it on. I use different tactics to deliver my message of 'build your personal brand' across different platforms, but the message itself doesn't change. Social media is a lot like speaking different languages. You need to understand how to translate your message into a medium that makes the most sense on that platform – you wouldn't (and can't) post a text post on YouTube. So, for example, on LinkedIn I might say 'Hello', but on TikTok I would say 'Bonjour', and on Instagram I'd say 'Konichiwa'. I am saying 'hi' the same on each platform, but the way I say it is contextual to the platform I am sharing it on. To build your reputation successfully you have to be consistent in your messaging, but make sense to the platform you're trying to share that message on.

Stick to your strategy

Once you have decided on your core message, stick to it. Don't fall into the trap of chasing trends or copying what other people have done. You could follow the Steven Bartlett, Gary Vee or Amelia Sordell playbook, and, you know what? You would probably get some traction. But would you build a personal brand? Nope. Because you are not Steven Barlett, or Gary Vee or me. None of us got to where we are by ripping off other people's strategies and stories – we are who we say we are and are unapologetic about that. Which is why people follow us. Your personal brand is your personal experience. Clue is in the name, it's personal. That's something you can't replicate – no matter how closely you copy our content. You can replicate how someone does something, but you can't copy *why* they do it that way – and it's each of our individual stories that's essential for creating friends rather than followers.

Basically, what I'm saying is that it's important to learn from other people's content and to observe what's working – this is how you can use trends to your advantage by spotting what type of content is getting the most traction on specific platforms and leaning into it – but behind whatever medium you use to share your message, the message has to be the same. And it has to be yours.

Getting Klowt: putting the heart into HR

Let me introduce you to Sarah, an HR consultant. When she started working with me, she had just under 3,000 followers on her LinkedIn account and was well aware that HR has a reputation for being. . . maybe a bit boring? However, the way she thinks about HR is so different to what many employees and business owners expect from someone in that role.

Sarah is driven by a need to make a positive impact on both the people in the organisations she works with, and also on her clients, who are the founders and leaders of those organisations. Why? Well, she's had her own experience of working in a toxic environment, and wants to prevent that for others. During one of our early one-to-one sessions, we discussed how we could turn her passion for change into a core message that would help both employees and business leaders understand that Sarah takes a slightly different approach to HR. It was tricky to strike the balance at first – I mean, HR is the department you only call when there is someone to fire. But then we landed on *the* message: that Sarah was putting the heart back in HR and driving the reinvention of HR's, quite frankly, lame reputation.

Her strategy then became all about positioning herself as an alternative to traditional HR. The opposite to what you'd expect. Sure, we still created content about onboarding, offboarding, hiring, firing, contracts and a load of other topics that you might consider necessary as a business owner, but also quite boring – but by doing it through the 'reinventing HR's lame reputation' lens we presented this information in a fun, human and often sassy way. Unsurprisingly, she built a significant LinkedIn following.

We started working together in 2022, and by late 2023, she had 22,000 followers on LinkedIn, many of whom fall into the 'friends vs. followers' category. Her content has been seen by more than 10 million people. Plus, she has won business off the back of her content, including paid speaking gigs.

Sarah's story shows exactly how a strong personal brand, and, of course, a foolproof strategy, can have a huge impact on you – both as an individual and on your business. Once it gets going, your personal brand content should pave the way for other content creation opportunities – like the speaking gigs Sarah attracted – because this is how you expand your reach even further, making more and more connections and inspiring more and more people.

Click moments

It's *so* much easier to create your strategy once you're clear on your 'why'. You need to be able to see where you want to be to plot the roadmap from where you are now to get there. In short, you reverse-engineer your route to success from the destination, not the start. A bit like a SatNav. Just don't lose sight of the entire point of this exercise – be personal. No one wants to follow a perfectly polished robot.

4

Challenge the norm

Stop being so vanilla. I say this a lot, and for good reason. How many times have you been in line at an ice cream shop and scanned the chocolate chip, the salted caramel, the Nocciola (. . . I eat Gelato) and thought 'forget mint choc chip or raspberry ripple! I'd really love some vanilla'? Vanilla isn't exciting. It's not interesting and it's certainly not giving the main character energy that mint choc chip gives. People don't buy vanilla, and if they do, it's because it's an accompaniment to a fancy dessert. So unless you want to be a side dish in life, don't be vanilla.

It's the same with your personal branding content. Sure, you could play it safe and post some mediocre stuff and it would be *fine*. But it wouldn't be, would it? Because you're not reading this book to be fine. You're reading this book to be excellent, and to leverage your excellence to unlock all the opportunities you want and deserve. So, that is why you need to put your big pants on and embrace the unique person and personality that you are, and be OK with people preferring someone else's flavour of content over yours.

To build a strong personal brand, you have to differentiate yourself from the millions of other people posting online. You have to embrace who you are, and be 100% OK with the consequences of being yourself. Do you think raspberry ripple gives a damn that people don't like it? No. It's raspberry ripple. Because for every person that doesn't like raspberry ripple, there is another who loves it. You can't say that about vanilla.

I know what you're thinking: how do I make authentic, unique content when social media platforms are already packed to the brim with really authentic creators? Well, you have a super power; the thing that makes you different from anyone else on this planet – you. A huge reason why people are able to grow so quickly on social media is they bring who they are to the table. If you don't highlight your personality through your content – which, scary as it sounds, might mean saying things that other people disagree with – then you are missing the point of personal branding. Growing your personal brand means standing out from the crowd – if you're afraid to do that, then your personal brand won't gain any traction.

All the time I see people who are investing time, money and energy into their personal brand only to get frustrated by the lack of results. The reason? They are unwilling to just *be themselves* online. (Sound familiar?) We know what this boils down to, right? It's because you're scared of being judged. You're scared of people seeing the real you and being rejected for it. And I get it, but here's the deal – I'm not going to try and pacify that anxiety by telling you that if you just let your true colours shine through, everyone will fall in love with you. Because they won't. Some people will think you're insufferable (just check my TikTok comments). But everyone falling in love with you is not real life.

You will almost certainly encounter critics online when you start putting yourself out there more, and you will likely receive feedback you would prefer not to hear. But it's rarely mean, and instead of being scared of someone disagreeing with you, embrace it. In my opinion, the best part of my personality is that it repels people whom I want to repel, and attracts the people I want to attract. It's like a sieve, but you won't have that natural filter if you're trying to please everybody.

You have to embrace the fact that some people aren't going to like you. Not even Mother Teresa was universally liked. There were people who accused her of navel-gazing, and of only doing good deeds so that people would think she was great. This isn't something that's limited to what you'll experience when you start working on your personal brand – this is life.

Of course, if this is all new to you – it's not going to be easy at first. But just remember that the reason you're taking control of your personal brand isn't because you want to win a popularity contest, but because you want to attract the opportunities that you deserve. Don't let your ego get in the way of that.

Another way to flip this around is to ask yourself, do you like everyone you encounter, either in real life or online? I'm pretty confident your answer to that question will be 'no'. And that's OK. You don't need everyone to like you, you just need the *right* people to like you. Don't shy away from polarisation – it can be a wonderful thing when it helps you 'sieve out' the wrong people and find the ones who will support you on your journey.

If you're adding flavour, make sure people can taste it

Back to vanilla ice cream. You're in a parlour, you've ordered your ice cream – gelato for me, please. You've sat down on a nice bench in the sun to enjoy it, ready to feel the impending sugar rush hit your veins. You take the first lick and. . . hmm, it doesn't really taste of anything? You keep eating it. . . Still nothing! Will you be raving to your friends about the parlour? Posting about it on Instagram? Going back every weekend? Absolutely not. What a disappointment.

A let-down. A catastrophe. I cannot imagine anything worse than spending all that time working, saving my pennies to buy an ice cream only for it to taste like nothing.

Your personal branding content is the same thing. If you're going to add flavour, you need to go all-in, otherwise, what's the point? Social media moves so quickly, without an opinion it'll just be forgotten. Or worse, never even see the light of day.

A good way to avoid tasteless content is asking yourself 'what's the f**king point?' every time you create a piece of content. It's something I always keep front-of-mind. In fact, it's one of the things we do at Klowt – we call it our 'Klowt filter'. It's kind of like an acid test of whether or not a post is worth posting. Your content should have enough flavour and context in it to answer the question 'what's the f**king point?' without you having to answer that out loud. You should be able to tell why something is being posted without needing an additional explanation.

If you're going to decide to have some flavour (please do), make sure that you're putting the right *ingredients* into your content – balancing all the flavours to make a content that looks, sounds and acts just like YOU. And that flavour will be different for everyone. In fact, it's important that it is! Some of us are really data-led, others very reactive in our opinions, some use stories to share their content, others will stand on a hill about things that most people really disagree with. Think of politicians. In short, if you're going to have flavour, own it. And be OK with the repercussions. Just look at Ryanair. Their whole brand strategy is built around taking the mick out of their customers. They know they're not for everyone, and they own it.

Create a 'no-fly' list

As I said earlier in this book, creating an honest and authentic personal brand doesn't mean that you have to talk about every single little detail of your life online. There are, for sure, topics that you can avoid. In fact, before you *even start* working on your personal brand, I'd grab a pad and pen – or the Notes app in your phone – and spend a few minutes making a list of areas you want to steer clear of. I call this a 'no-fly' list – and what goes on there will be different for everyone. Some people will have their children on this list, others will have politics or religion. In some cases, it could be even more specific – such as not talking about the recently-exited co-founder of your business. There are plenty of things on my 'no-fly' list – my kids' faces, where I live, the car I drive, my opinions on politics. You can build a personal brand without being private. And not talking about some things in my private life hasn't negatively impacted my ability to grow an incredibly successful personal brand.

Getting Klowt: the stranger on the Tube

I had an awkward moment on my commute recently. On my way into work, a man on the Tube came over to me and said, 'Hi Amelia! It's me, Steve! Nice to see you.' My mind went into overdrive. Where did I know this guy from? Was he an ex-colleague? A friend of a friend? I was mentally trying to place him as I replied with a friendly, 'Hi, Steve, nice to see you too. . .'

We had a brief conversation but as I stepped off the train I still had no idea where I'd met him before.

Then my phone buzzed – I had a message from Steve on LinkedIn. 'Hi, Amelia, it was me on the Tube earlier. So nice to meet you, I've been following you for years!' That was when the penny dropped – this wasn't someone I'd met before in real life, but it *was* someone

(continued)

who had been following and commenting on my content for months. I didn't know him at all, but he was convinced he knew me because he sees my content every day - that's why he greeted me as a friend.

I'd created a genuine relationship with him using my content - and I'd done it without oversharing the details of my life that I want to keep private. In fact, what he sees online is probably a maximum of 10% of who I am as a person. It's concrete proof that posting authentic content is genuinely *so* impactful - and that you don't need to go into the gory details of your life to grow your personal brand successfully.

You are a big, glistening iceberg. What you share as content is just the tiny tip that sticks out above the surface of the ocean – but there is a whole lot more under the water that most people never see.

In many ways, this is no different to the fact that you are a different person at work to the one you are at home. I've had friends tell me that the way I come across on LinkedIn is very different to who I am as a person – my response is always that they are also probably different in a work environment than they are with their friends and family. (The 'you' who gives boardroom updates about key performance indicators (KPIs) is probably not the same 'you' who plays board games in your pyjamas with your kids. . . or rants in the pub on a Friday night with your best friend.) This dichotomy is something that most of us are used to navigating in the workplace, but that we can find harder to balance when it comes to personal branding.

The key is to remember that you need to be strategic – the content you share is designed to *shape* your reputation. It's a good idea to take a breath before hitting publish on posts – take a few minutes to simply ask yourself whether the post you're about to publish is in line with your strategy. Does it positively build and protect your reputation as the person in your space? If the answer is yes, post it. If the answer is no, don't.

Finding the balance between personal and private

I'm not saying that you *can't* build a successful personal brand by sharing your private life. I mean, the Kardashians are pretty incredible examples of people who have built powerhouse personal brands by sharing every single aspect of their lives. (Including their boyfriends, salad orders and sister punch-ups.) The thing is, you have to find the balance that will best serve you. And that might change throughout your career and life.

Take, for example, Robbie Williams. The Netflix documentary he released in 2023 went through the deepest, darkest chapters of his life – his drug addiction, his sex addiction, cheating on his girlfriend, even having steroid injections just to be able to get on stage and perform each night. Arguably, if he'd taken us on that journey when he was at the height of his career, no one would have trusted him enough to listen to his music. But now he's reached a level of influence where he's able to be open – and we all loved that he shared those incredibly personal and private parts of his story.

I do this. I will share content, reflecting on things I've done and mistakes I've made. But I probably wouldn't do that in real time. Sometimes, sharing what's private can create intimacy and build a relationship with your audience. Other times? It can have the opposite effect and actually alienate your followers. In 2022, a CEO shared a photo of himself crying and accompanied it with a post complaining about how hard his job was – the LinkedIn community aptly named him The Crying CEO (God, I love the internet). The post went viral and created a lot of backlash – he shared too much in real time and created a lack of trust between him and his followers. More importantly, his post would also have made his team (of about 200 people) question whether or not he was actually a decent boss.

The crying and finding his job hard aren't actually the bad thing – and doing so in front of his friends or family would have been completely acceptable. I joked to my team today about my 'scheduled crying' (I say joke, it's half-joking). But sharing a crying selfie on LinkedIn just comes across as attention-seeking. And, quite honestly, unhinged. Not things you want to be portraying with your personal brand. Remember what I said about protecting your reputation? He needed a 'what's the f**king point?' filter put on this before he hit 'post'.

Basically, we all have to find our own balance between what's personal and what's private. I've already told you that you need to share some of your personality online, but that doesn't mean you have to share *all* of yourself online. But most of us fall into the camp of holding too much back – we often aren't happy to share every detail of our lives online. And, guess what? That's totally fine. Not all of us want to be a Kardashian. . .

The real key is being a human in your content – and, in my experience, the reason *most* people fail to get traction with their personal brands is not because they have too much personality, it's because they have a lack of it.

Fatal flaws for a personal brand

Fatal flaws. Definition: *A flaw which causes an otherwise noble or exceptional character to bring about their own downfall and, often, their eventual death.* OK, so maybe the death bit is a bit dramatic, but you get my drift. Here are some of the things that will block you from actually building a strong personal brand and getting all those wonderful opportunities you deserve:

1. Overthinking it.

2. Thinking you have to be 'smart' to be valuable.

3. Not knowing who your audience is.

4. Not knowing which channel(s) to post on.

5. Not engaging with others.

6. Inconsistency.

7. Trying to talk about everything.

Overthinking it

When I first started building my personal brand, it would take me hours to write a post because I was so worried about people not liking it. I would carefully caveat every opinion I had, I'd structure posts in a way that felt 'perfect' only for it to be liked by three people. The honest truth was I was completely overthinking my content, and how it was perceived online.

The reality is, social media moves really quickly. So does life. And if you're spending hours on a single post that is only going to be seen or read for seven seconds, you've wasted hours. Building a personal brand is a marathon, not a sprint, and not every run is going to be a personal best. And, I get it, posting content is scary. Trying to take control of your reputation and personal brand is scary, but if you overthink everything, you will never post anything.

One of the things I say to my team at Klowt is 'Done well is always better that perfect.' And I mean it. Because perfect never gets done. Perfect is another word for procrastination. You can't benefit from something you've never executed, and if you don't share what you actually want to share, how will you ever know whether or not it's worth sharing? Overthinking your content and your personal brand removes the personality, it removes the humanity and waters you down. Do you want to be a watered-down version of yourself? No? Stop overthinking it then, and just f**king post it.

The other side of this coin is a lack of confidence. I certainly wasn't confident when I first started – quite the opposite. I used to second-guess myself in all areas of my life. Every interaction I had with people I'd go over in my head, analysing whether or not I'd sounded stupid. But a wonderful byproduct of building my personal brand and just taking that leap is that I am now 100% OK with the consequences of being myself. I am really happy with who I am as a person, and therefore I don't overthink anything any more. I am secure.

Building your confidence is a lot like learning to swim as a kid. When you first get in the water, you have armbands, a life jacket and a float or one of those fun little noodles. As you get more confident, the armbands come off, then the life jacket. Eventually, you take the float away and you're swimming about unaided, having a whale of a time. This is all about confidence, though, and nothing to do with ability – we have the ability and muscle strength to swim unaided as a baby, but we don't have the confidence. Building your confidence both online and off, is the same.

And why do you become so much more confident through taking control of your personal brand? Through building resilience. Through owning who you are and through each time you post, becoming slightly more authentic to the point where I am now. . . . Genuinely not caring about other people's opinions of my opinions (I do care about what people think about my character, but we'll get into that later). Putting in the reps, day in, day out, of owning your story and your opinions online gradually toughens you up in the best way. For now, though? Regardless of how confident (or not) you feel, you need to understand that if you really want to be seen as *the* person in your space, you're going to have to start posting content. And through posting that content you will begin to feel more confident. So put your big pants on and get to work.

Thinking you have to be 'smart' to be valuable

I think one of the biggest mistakes you can make in building your personal brand is thinking that every piece of content you share needs to make you look intelligent. Intelligence doesn't make you valuable. I follow plenty of meme accounts that will prove that. What you really need to do to build a big and strong personal brand is to be valuable to the audience you're trying to reach. You need to know what their pain points are, their lifestyles, their dreams – what is going to resonate with them, and pull that lever over and over again. And that could look like an in-depth analysis of cognitive dissonance, or a meme of a little girl standing outside a house on fire. Both are valuable to different people.

When it comes to content specifically, and communication generally, to be honest, the best way to approach things is: communicate complex ideas, simply. Because people don't buy complexity, they buy simplicity. Even brain surgeons, scrolling through LinkedIn looking for information are going to scroll right past your content on neurotransmitters because it's boring as hell. You've used too many jargon words, added more text than required because you're trying to look smart. Well, that isn't going to build you a brand, my friend, because if your content is so overwhelmingly boring no one reads it, you'll never build the traction you need to build anything. So even if you have a PhD, you need to understand that communicating complex ideas simply is why people love social media – it's short-form communication.

You have around three seconds to hook people in and around seven seconds total before they disengage on the micro-content platforms like TikTok, Instagram and LinkedIn. So, if you're writing like you're sending a White Paper to NASA, you've already lost. A good rule of thumb is to look at it like this, could a 12-year-old read and understand this? Yes? Good. No? You need to do more work to simplify it. Trust me, genuinely smart people don't need to overcomplicate things to get their point across. You are also genuinely smart, so use those smarts to cut out the fluff and share your ideas in a simple format that makes sense online.

There's another point here: copying and rewording other people's content, because you think they look and sound smart. They look and sound smart, because they are. You copying their content makes you look dumb. Avoid this at all costs. I promise, it's not going to help you – the person you're copying will have completely different goals to you. Probably a different audience and, let's be honest, you're not the same person. That is why personal branding is so great – we all bring different things to the table.

It's so important to be clear about your goals for growing your personal brand – when you know what you're aiming to achieve, you can leverage *your* personal experience, *your* knowledge and *your* opinions to reach the people you need to reach to make those goals happen. Without having to steal other people's words.

As I've said already in this book, in order to attract the right audience, you also need to be super super clear about who that audience is. If you are not specific about who you're talking to and what you're talking to them about, you'll end up talking about everything – your top tips for making Yorkshire puddings, how you learned karate, last night's *Friends* rerun. . . There's a reason for the saying, 'jack of all trades, master of none'. People won't take you seriously if you throw your net too wide. More on that in a second.

Take me as an example – I want to be known as an expert in personal branding, so I talk about it a lot. I've been able to create a very successful personal brand because I'm very clear about who I need to attract and therefore what I need to talk about – and the value I need to provide. Sometimes it's practical advice on personal branding, other times it's a meme about trolls being mean to you because they're actually insecure.

Both are valuable, one makes me look smart, the other makes me look, hopefully, like I have a sense of humour. Next flaw. . .

Not knowing who your audience is

You know what you want to be known for – now you need to work out *who* you can help with your knowledge and expertise. This is your audience! While I was writing this book, a client on the Get Klowt personal branding platform told me he wanted to be known as a social media expert, a talent manager *and* a football coach. My first question to him was, 'How on earth do you expect to find people who want to get *all of those things* from just *one* person?' He told me that he didn't, so then I asked him who his audience was. His answer was, 'I don't know.' That's not uncommon – but it's a fatal error! *Properly* get to know your goal and know who you need to build relationships with to reach that goal – then you'll be onto a winner.

Get clear on your goals, work out who you need to attract to make those goals happen. When you know the answers, you'll have a much better idea of who you need in your audience, and therefore what 'value' you need to provide for them.

Not knowing which channel(s) to post on

Let me just get one thing clear, there is no 'best' channel for building your personal brand. There is only the best channel to reach your intended audience. I hate it when I see online 'gurus' and coaches promoting specific platforms for reach and engagement, because it doesn't matter if you go viral on LinkedIn if everyone you're trying to sell to is on Instagram. An easy way to get to the bottom of this, quickly, is either ask your intended audience – speak to a client, customer, or send a few messages to ideal audience profile fits on social and ask them where they spend their time. Which channels do they live on? Then start there. Or, do what I do, because I don't have the patience for that kind of primary research, Google 'What is the best social media channel to reach [your audience]?' and you'll find loads of articles and resources telling you where to go. Or even better, fill out the personal branding strategy assessment when you sign up to the Get Klowt platform and it will tell you exactly which channel you need to build on.

It's also important that you don't try to post on too many channels at once – especially when you're just starting out. I built my personal brand exclusively on LinkedIn for three years before I even considered using any other platforms. Why? If you try to post on too many, you'll either get overwhelmed by the volume of content you need to create – and probably give up – or you'll dilute your message so much that no one will give a monkey's about what you have to say.

My advice is to focus on one channel first – the one that will make the biggest impact. My main focus is to reach B2B entrepreneurs, founders and executives, which is why I picked LinkedIn. My secondary goal was to reach the 'ring of influence' around those people, and help them grow their personal brands too. That's why I now *also* post on TikTok, YouTube and Instagram. But I didn't create content for any of those platforms until I'd absolutely nailed LinkedIn.

Just like over-analysing your content, worrying too much about building across every channel is also a waste of your time and energy – *and* is likely to damage your chances of getting the compound effect you're seeking. You might even end up changing your strategy before you've given it time to see if it will work. Big mistake. So start where your audience are spending the most time. And only once you've built up a cadence and traction on that channel, do you start looking at others.

Not engaging with others

Personal branding is not about talking *at* people, it's about talking *with* them. About articulating messages that make people look and read your content and see themselves in what you're saying. If you're not actively engaging with other people's content, and replying to comments and conversations on your own, you're missing a huge piece of this personal branding puzzle.

If you want engagement, you have to give it. It's like an ecosystem. People want to engage with other people who they know they're going to get a response from, so make a list of thought leaders, influencers and people who have audiences of people you're trying to reach – it doesn't have to be people from your industry, ideally, it's not. It just needs to be people who have audiences you can benefit from reaching, and spend time commenting on their posts every day. A good hack here is add a calendar invite to your diary for around the time of when you post and spend 10–15 minutes just engaging with other people's stuff.

From my personal branding playbook: the 10 × 3 rule

Find 10 thought leaders and influencers in your space.

Find 10 recent posts from those people to comment on.

Spend 10 minutes commenting on 10 different posts.

Inconsistency

Building a personal branding is 10% great content and 90% consistency in posting it. If you get distracted and have 'shiny new object' syndrome for every new trend, topic, thing going – you will fail to get any traction. Be steadfast in your message, and flexible in your mediums to share it. Test and iterate, work out what works for each platform and also hacks you can use to grow, but maintain the integrity of your personal branding message and the consistency in which you're sharing it, always.

It's like going to the gym. You don't say you want the sexiest body of your life and then go for three weeks and say it's not working, or worse, give up. I posted for nearly 12 months before I saw any real traction – but once I did, I was getting millions of views a month. So hang in there.

Trying to talk about everything

Let me tell you something, you don't have to have an opinion on everything. In fact, you only really *have* to talk about one thing – what you want to be known for. Being clear on the topics you need to talk about to attract your audience means that you won't ever fall into the trap of thinking you need to discuss everything.

There's also a more granular detail here which is, your content doesn't need to say everything either. One of the things I see people do is have an interesting topic they want to talk about – it's bang on for their audience, but they give their audience no room to comment or engage because they've caveated and considered all perspectives, objections, challenges and opinions in their post. Don't do that. You want to start a conversation, not have one with yourself. If you want to say more than one thing, turn the idea into multiple posts. Remember what I said about communicating complex ideas simply? If you're trying to say too much, you're overcomplicating it.

A way in which I tend to structure content, both written and video for social media, is what we call the Klowt Kontent Sandwich. Imagine the most delicious sandwich you've ever seen. Delicious, crusty bread and loads of delicious fillings.

- The first piece of bread in your sandwich is your hook. This is what people are going to see before they bite into the deeper bit of what you have to say.

- The second layer is your filling. This is your context, your expansion on whatever your hook was.

- And the final layer is the second piece of bread. This is what you use to engage your audience and encourage them to respond – 'what do you think?', 'agree?' You'll have seen people use these as a call to conversation in content, because they work.

Click moments

Personal branding is meant to be, well, personal. Which means you have to bring your personality and the thing that makes you unique to the table, but that doesn't mean you have to share every tiny detail of your life online. Think about what the impact of sharing certain details will have – create your 'no fly' list and go from there. Remember, if it doesn't help you meet your goal, then it's not worth posting.

5

Finding friends not followers

When you first start building your personal brand, there's an easy mistake that most people make. Thinking that it's all about *you*. Focusing all your content and activities on trying to sell whatever it is you want people to buy, whether that's a product or service, 'buy' you as an employer or a potential employee. For example, you want to get CEOs to buy accountancy services, therefore you post content, speaking specifically to CEOs about accountancy services. Boring. And also, strategically speaking, dumb.

Why is this dumb? Because no one wants to be sold to, and they most certainly do not want to read content selling them accountancy services. Furthermore, nine times out of ten, the clients who find me and Klowt, don't find us through my personal branding content. They find us through content I share about the challenges of running a business, the mistakes I've made, the frustrations, wins, trials and tribulations about being an adult with responsibilities. The reason they pay Klowt for personal brandings services after seeing this content is because they resonate with it. They can see themselves in what I am sharing, which creates a connection. So when they are ready to buy personal branding services – or accountancy services – the person they feel that connection with is who they're going to buy from. Make sense?

Most people think far too literally about who their audience is and what they're trying to 'sell' to them. And so they end up just constantly forcing this kind of content down their throat. Have you ever been cold-called before? Ick. Well, that is how your content is coming across. Think for a moment about the people on the street soliciting donations for charities – I don't think there's been a single time I've stopped to talk to one of those people when they've tried to approach me. It's not because I don't want to give money to charity – I try to be as generous as I can. I don't stop because I know they're going to try and *sell* to me. And *no one wants to be sold to*, but *everyone wants to buy*.

When the only type of content you're posting is hard sales stuff, it has the same 'repelling' effect. In fact, it doesn't just stop people engaging with your content, it actually makes them run away from it – and your personal brand. Huge mistake! The solution? Encouraging people to buy from you without coming across as salesy. Easy, right?

This might surprise you, but in the three and a half years I've been running Klowt, I've only asked people directly to buy what we're selling in my content about THREE times – that's out of hundreds and hundreds of posts. My business is built entirely on inbound leads and to date we've generated around $1 million in revenue through that content. People buy from people, but more importantly – in our heavily commoditised world – they buy from people they *like and trust*. But how do you build that trust with an audience of people you've never actually met in real life? Well, it goes back to what I was saying earlier about sharing content and ideas that create resonance with your ideal audience. Focus on how many *relationships* you can build with those people, rather than how many *followers* you have – aka, find friends, not followers. You need to build rapport – that comes from talking about multiple aspects of our lives, not just what you're selling.

Look back at the section on rings of influence in Chapter 3 for an example of how this works – as I mentioned then, I post content aimed at executive assistants (EAs), because I know that these people are the gatekeepers for the CEOs I want to reach.

Come back to your why

Only when you are clear on your why and your overarching goal for taking control of your personal brand, will who you need to target become clear. The bottom line is, if you're not clear on your goal, it's very, very difficult to figure out who you need to attract to make that goal happen. (If you've completed the exercise I shared in Chapter 2, you will already have a stronger idea of who your audience needs to be.)

Let's take me as an example, I am growing my personal brand because I want to be known for personal branding on the mainstream stage. I want Steven Bartlett or Tony Robbins-level notoriety. Recognised-in-the-street-type-stuff. However, for me to make that happen, I need to generate business. Why? This is what will allow me to do everything I need to do to achieve that bigger goal. And the people who buy my services are typically executives, founders and marketing teams, who are looking to find a way to build a brand for their executives or founders.

From that goal, and my strategy to get there, I know that I have three main audiences:

- The everyman, who I need to get in front of to become 'mainstage famous'.

- Executives and founders who want to grow their personal brands.

- Marketing teams who need someone to help their executives and founders develop their personal brands.

The everyman audience might sound extremely broad – but there are still opportunities for me to resonate with people by talking about different aspects of my life. On a human level, we all have the same problems and dreams. We all want to live a nice, relatively comfortable life, doing the things we love. We all want to be happy, meet the love of our lives and die with no regrets. When I break it down in those terms, it's easy to see how pulling on those levers will help me resonate with loads of people outside the narrower demographic who will actually buy my services.

This is why I post content about my divorce, life being tough, business failures and personal screw-ups. It's the vulnerable honesty that not only makes people remember me, but also makes people like and trust me. But know this – *even if* those people like and trust me, it doesn't mean they're going to spend $6,000 per month with Klowt. For that, I need to reach the CEOs. And that's why I post content about being a business founder too – I share stories about my first business failure, how I discovered a $100,000 hole in my revenue last year and all the other challenges I've faced as an executive trying to scale a business.

You might think that if I want to be known for personal branding, the logical approach would be to only talk about personal branding, but this won't reach or resonate with other founders in the same way. Many of them might not be interested in content about personal branding, but they will resonate with tales about being a business founder. By sharing my stories from the perspective of being a founder, I draw them into my content – and once they're there, over time, I indirectly position myself to them as an expert in personal branding. By posting content that they can see themselves in, I build relationships at scale. . . and obtain followers, which positions me as an expert in personal branding. So, when they are ready to buy what I'm selling, the connection is there, and so is the proof of concept that I know what I'm doing. They're not buying from a stranger, they're buying from a trusted *friend*.

One caveat to add about my 'everyman' audience – I did not start out with the intention to create content for everyone. This audience has become part of my wider strategy because, I'm going to be honest, I want to be famous. Judge me, I don't care. At least I'm honest. The reason I want to be famous is in part for my ego, sure, but mainly because the more people who know who I am, the more I can spread my messages of being 100% OK with the consequences of being yourself, being unafraid of failure and encouraging people to build their brand.

I needed a role model when I was younger to boost my confidence and tell me it was all going to work out. I want to be that role model for other people which is very hard to do if no one knows who you are. However, I would not be where I am now if I'd started with an 'everyman' audience as part of my strategy. The only reason I'm able to now target the majority is because I spent years with a laser focus on sharing personal branding content and becoming the go-to person in that niche.

You certainly shouldn't try to appeal to everyone at the start of your personal branding journey, because if you try to appeal to everyone, you end up appealing to no-one. If you want to be known as an authority in your space, channel your focus there.

Find the right niche

It's so important to find the right content niche. If you want to be *famous*, you have to be famous for *something*. But don't make the mistake of taking that literally – a recruiter who sells recruitment services might think their niche is recruitment, but just posting about recruitment isn't actually going to get you the audience (friends) you need to win business and attract candidates.

In fact, a recruiter's niche isn't recruitment at all, it's the experiences of people who work in a specific industry that the recruiter targets.

Let's say you want to be the best software development recruiter in the world. If you only talk about software development recruiting, the only people you're going to attract with your content are *other recruiters*. And they're not going to pay your bills. If you talk about the challenges of getting a job as a software developer, the state of the market, champion candidates' experiences and good employers, you will attract software developers and hiring managers in that space. Speak to them about what they care about, not what you do for a living.

The whole point of this is to attract people into your network by getting them to see themselves in your content. Talking intimately about their aspirations, dreams, challenges, pain and wins means they feel understood. Like you get them. And that will separate you from every single other person in your space, making you *the* option, not just an option among many.

Tips for finding your niche

Let's quickly talk about audience profiles. Most of you – especially if you're in marketing – will spend too much time on this. The reality is, there are only a few things that really matter when defining your audience.

Who do you sell to? And I don't mean 'B2B' or 'salespeople'. I mean *who* do you actually sell to? What's their job title or function within an organisation (if that's relevant)? Is it people working in procurement? Do you sell to sales directors? What do *they* dream about? What are *their* biggest concerns? What stresses *them* out? What are *their* needs? Keep asking those questions until you've a clear idea of who that person is, and what they give a s**t about.

It's only by knowing *exactly* who you sell to that you can work out what you need to talk about to get them interested in *you*.

And if that still baffles you, ask them. If you genuinely don't know what to talk about to attract the people you need to attract, find some of them and ask them directly. Jump on LinkedIn or Instagram – search for your ideal audience and send them a Direct Message. If you already have an established career in your space and are already selling to these people, contact five of your favourite clients and say, 'I'm going to be starting to share content online, would you mind if I asked you a few questions? I'm happy to pay for your time.' (Bonus tip: offering payment shows you respect their time – and more often than not the other person will agree to talk to you for 30 minutes and but won't ever ask for a fee. Ask them for a straight favour? They'll almost always say no.)

There are two advantages to having these conversations. The first is that you'll get detailed, valuable information about what the people you're trying to attract actually care about. The second is that they'll feel like you're trying to get to know them better – it feeds their ego. That's only going to strengthen your relationships – and your personal brand. Of course, there is a limit to how many times you can have these kinds of chats, particularly when you're starting out, so my second little trick is to include a couple of these questions in your calls with clients or prospects. This could be a hiring manager, or candidate too, by the way.

When I first started proactively building my personal brand, I'd add a series of questions to the end of every call with a prospect or someone who was part of my ideal audience. I'd ask them things like, 'What's the biggest challenge that you're facing right now in your role or business?' and 'Why did you get into the industry? What has made you stay?' This was incredibly valuable because, firstly, my ideal audience was giving me first-hand detail of what they were interested in that allowed me to create incredible tailored and relatable content. But, secondly, it meant the people I was asking these questions to felt like I was genuinely interested in what they had to say – I was – and so further cemented our bond and relationship. It was an excellent networking *and* personal branding play.

Take the example I made earlier with the software development recruiter, if you were them, you might ask prospective clients, 'Just out of interest, what made you join your company?' and 'What's been the biggest challenge you've had while you guys have been scaling?' The answers about desires and frustrations = great personal branding content. And once you ask those questions three, four, five times? You'll be razor clear on who your audience is and what they care about – that is what will win you *friends*, not followers. And build an incredibly successful personal brand in your niche.

Bonus tip to get even more insight from your ideal audience. Ask them who are the thought leaders they like – and on what platforms they follow them. This gives you a list of people who you can follow and engage with to attract more audience members, just like that potential customer, into your network. Work smarter, not harder.

Levelling up when building your audience

There are different levels to personal branding. Level one is posting a piece of content online, level ten is getting paid to speak at an industry conference or event – level one hundred, you're Beyoncé.

If you're at level one, just getting content out there on the right social platform is enough. Set a key performance indicator (KPI) of how many times a week to post, and strive to hit it. One of the reasons we set up the Get Klowt platform was to solve this problem – it asks you a bunch of questions and spits out a personal branding strategy, including how many times you should be posting and on what channel to reach your ideal customer.

At level two, you want to start thinking about optimising that content, making sure it's actually helping you achieve your goals. Like, what is performing well and what gets crickets? Do more of the former and less of the latter. And by level six? You'll be in a good cadence of posting, but people will start to get to know who you are and want to proactively mention your names in rooms you otherwise won't have access to. This is the tipping point of when all the work you've been doing starts to pay dividends. This is also when the rings of influence that I talked about in Chapter 3 come into play (figure 5.1). So, if your audience is at the centre of what you're doing, who forms the golden ring around those people? Who influences *them*?

This is why my third main audience is people working in marketing, not because I work with them directly, but because they are the gatekeepers to the entrepreneurs, executives and founders who I *do* work with. It's marketers who are most likely to come across my content and introduce me to people who could become my clients. And sign off budget to pay for it.

So, hypothetically, if your clients are high-net-worth individuals, you are likely to want to appeal to EAs. That might mean you could share a piece of content about how hard EAs work or how they're grossly undervalued. Even though EAs aren't going to buy your services, they are the ones who can get you in front of the people who will.

Figure 5.1: The ring of influence.

However, you need to make sure you don't muddy the waters by constantly posting about EAs – they aren't your target audience. You need to take a more holistic view of your content and think about who is in the circle of trust around your ideal client, and how you can access them without distracting from your core message.

For example, instead of just posting about the trials and tribulations a decision-maker might have, you could post about some of the trials and tribulations a decision-maker might have *that could impact the people in their circle of trust.* Take our software recruiter – you could post about when a founder is under the pump to hire new people, how that stress impacts their team. You're still talking about something that impacts your ideal audience, but you're framing it in such a way that it will also be understood by the people *around* your ideal client. The ring of influence.

Let's look at an example outside of the corporate realm. Let's say you're a life coach who specialises in men's mental health. You've realised that often the men who come to you have been encouraged to do so by people close to them. Maybe a spouse, a partner, a friend. From this, you know you're not only speaking to the men you want to help, but also their *ring of influence* as well. Your content becomes a roughly 50/50 split between adding value to the men you want to help and championing the people around them.

When it comes to how you decide on the ratio of content directly targeting your ideal clients and the content targeting the people in their circle of trust, there is no definitive answer. My advice is to test and learn. Start with a 50/50 split, then go up to 60/40 in favour of your ideal client. Perhaps drop it to 30/70 as an experiment. See what lands best and what gets you the results you're looking for. As with every single piece of advice in this book, and in any other self-development book – you won't know unless *you* do it.

The main benefit to casting your net a little wider vs. exclusively focusing on one type of person is you're giving yourself the best shot of taking 'market share' in your niche. Eric Partaker is a great example of how to do this well on a platform like LinkedIn – all he does is talk about leadership, but he does it in such a way that it appeals to both the CEOs he offers coaching to *and* the people they employ. He knows that if he can appeal to employees, that will pull his content into the feeds of the CEOs he's selling to. *The ring of influence.*

When you think a bit more holistically about who you're trying to attract, you give yourself access to multiple doors into your ideal audience – and into making money vs. trying to bang on the front door. Do this and growth will happen more quickly, you'll get better engagement and this, in turn, will give you access to more people and put more eyes on your profile, which can only be a good thing! Basically, it's the fast-track to more and better opportunities. Who doesn't want that? But be warned, this is for levelling up your brand. If you're reading this book, starting at level one – turn the page corner and put a note in your diary to come back to this in three to four months' time. Do not talk to everyone when you first start – otherwise you'll get nowhere.

Don't limit yourself to your content

Don't wait for people to find you – go out and find *friends* yourself. One of the most underrated ways to grow an audience is to engage in other people's. And in my opinion if you want engagement, you have to be willing to give it first. Make a list of people you want to follow and whose content attracts audiences that you want access to, then send them a connection request or hit the follow button. Make it part of your routine. Maybe set a reminder to identify and connect with a few new people every week. (I find Friday afternoons are perfect for this kind of thing.) Reach out, say hi, compliment their content – you will not only find you attract new followers, but that these people *also* become friends. And that's the first step to creating community.

Bonus hack: Identify creators and thought leaders whose audiences are made up of similar people to those you're looking to attract. Pick up to ten of these people and spend five minutes engaging with their content each day. Ask questions, stir up discussions, share your opinions on hot topics, mention them in *your* content. Create community chatter on both their platform and your own. Get people talking – and do your best to keep your comments open to invite responses. And when people do comment? For the love of God, reply to them.

Click moments

Meaningful connections with the people you're interacting with – that's what should be front of mind when you're developing your personal brand. It's not about likes and views, it's about scaling your reputation. Always remember the mantra of finding friends *not* followers. Use the hacks in this chapter to start building a community of people who know who you are, what you stand for and – most importantly – who know, like and trust you. People want to do business with people they know, like and trust.

6

What are you known for?

To become famous, you have to be famous for something. Right? David Beckham is famous for football. Matthew McConaughey is famous for acting. Taylor Swift is famous for singing. Even the most 'talentless' reality TV stars are famous for breaking someone's heart on *Love Island* or giving an iconic diary B-roll interview on *Selling Sunset*. And yet, I almost guarantee at the start of this book, you have little idea of what *you* should be famous for. Maybe the word 'famous' even gives you the ick. If it does, you either need to put your big pants on and get over it, or put this book down and read something that makes you feel more comfortable. I am not here to soothe your imposter syndrome, or fear of visibility. I am here to help you build a personal brand. That might sound harsh, but if you aren't clear on what you want to be known for, how can you expect anyone to take you seriously as an expert or thought leader in your field – let alone trust you enough to *buy* from you?

When you first start out, you need focus. You need serious clarity on what you need to be known for and to whom in order to achieve your overarching goal. The 'what' is the core message behind your content. And ultimately what people will say about you in rooms you're not in, so knowing what you want them to say about you is pretty damn important (which is why, by the way, if you haven't yet got super-clear about *who* you want to talk to and *what you want to achieve* with your brand, you should go and do that *before* you start creating content – in fact, go and do that right now!).

Your core content pillars

I could sit here and give you tons of different ways to come up with your content pillars. We could call them core messages, pillars, values – I could pretend to be incredibly smart and use all my marketing lingo. But the reality is, the only thing you need to be able to build a solid foundation of a strong personal brand is clarity on what you want people to know you for. It really is that simple. And that is always why it is so hard.

These are my content pillars.

1. Personal branding.

2. My story.

The problem is, both of those overlap because building my personal brand *is* part of my story. So let me break it down into an easier formula. I talk about personal branding because that is what I *do*. I post content about my story because that is who I *am*. Both are valuable, both make you stand out – and both are required to get your name mentioned in rooms you otherwise wouldn't have access to.

The following are my content pillars and example subtopics underneath them:

1. Personal branding:

    a. Personal branding benefits.

    b. Personal branding on social media.

   c.   Tactics to build your personal brand.

   d.   How to create a podcast to build your personal brand.

2. My story.

   a.   Why I started building my personal brand.

   b.   Why failing has led me to succeed.

   c.   Some of the lessons I've learned growing my business.

   d.   What it's like being a single mum of two and trying to juggle a career, a team and a company.

No one is going to remember a mortgage broker that simply talks about mortgages. But they do remember a mortgage broker who talks about his journey getting into the industry after struggling to buy his first home with his pregnant wife. Makes sense? Your expertise is what people are buying, but your story is why they buy it from *you*. And when you get the balance between the two right, amazing things happen. You attract the audience you're trying to attract. They engage with you. They resonate with you. They buy from you. Not only is it good for business but it also gives you one heck of a confidence boost. It's like a reward for being brave enough to be yourself. And the best part? You personally and intrinsically feel like what you're sharing is aligned to who you are – and that is the inflection point of self-confidence, and a strong personal brand.

The subtopics of your overarching content pillars are the distribution of who you are. If I told you to 'talk about mortgages', you'd fatigue out in five posts. If I told you to Google the top 50 most searched terms surrounding mortgages, and answer those in posts AND then Google '50 things that people care about' and asked you to use those as inspiration for your own stories about your life and challenges, you'd have 100 days' worth of content for multiple channels. And if you can't be bothered to do that, sign up to Get Klowt at klowt.com/membership and our AI tool will tell you what to post, for both content pillars. It's why I created it in the first place.

Creating content isn't actually that hard, once you are clear on what you need to be talking about. As I said, the first pillar is what you *do*, the second is why people should buy that thing from *you*.

One thing I would say here is to make sure you don't ignore the humanity in your expertise content. Don't exclusively rely on giving 'valuable' information to build your brand. For example, if you were a copywriter and all you posted about was how to write good copy, that's boring. Bringing in your story – maybe a love of storytelling and a desire to make others fall in love with writing – means you never run out of things to say, and you have personal reasons for people to listen to you say it. A two-day content plan might involve analysing other people's copy, and explaining why it's good, with the next day explaining how you got into copywriting and why storytelling is important to you.

> Your expertise + your story/your audience
> = your personal brand.

This is the sweet spot. It's where you begin to blend your expertise with your values in your content. Posting not only becomes more enjoyable for you – it also resonates with your audience because you're teaching them how to become better copywriters.

Your core content pillars can be a statement, or a topic – for example, at Klowt we have one client who wants to be known as '*the* D2C (direct to consumer) guy', because he is the CEO of a large D2C business. D2C is all he talks about online. His content is bound by that clearly defined statement.

I have a statement as my core message too. 'To be the go-to person for personal branding'. *All* of my expertise content comes back to the themes of personal branding; how to do it, tactics, what I do, how I built mine, how to deal with negativity, being brave enough to hit 'post' – anything that ties in with that theme of personal branding. On the flip side, my story content is all centred around how I got to where I am, what I'm up to, failures, lessons, wins, trials and tribulations. I even vlog my life on YouTube. This is important because it's not enough to show people you're the best at what you do, you have to be the best known – and it's much easier to stand out when people get to know you as a person vs. relying on your skills alone.

The statement I use means something powerful to me, and it sits at the centre of my content creation. If you're emotive and empathetic, you're more likely to want a statement like me – the kind of thing that makes you feel hopeful and passionate – as your 'core message' or pillar. If you're cynical and pragmatic? You're going to want just a subject, like 'personal branding' – everyone has different motivations, so find what works for you.

Whether you have a subject or a statement for your core message doesn't matter – the key is that you have one area of focus. *One!* If you want to be known for *something*, you can't talk about *everything*. As soon as you start posting about more than one thing, you will struggle to build any kind of brand equity or become known as an individual with a specific area of expertise.

Focus on expertise, not being an expert

There's a difference between *expertise* and being an *expert*. Some people read the word expertise and think '*I'm not an expert, yet*'. But expertise isn't about *being* an expert – I actually think if you call yourself an expert, you're probably already behind. It's about where your experience, skills and knowledge lie. I probably wouldn't call myself an expert in personal branding, but I would say I'm someone who knows a lot about it and who, as a result, has expertise in that space.

You could be a graduate with expertise in social media, if you have spent time learning about different platforms and understanding them. You could be a 65-year-old retired firefighter who wants to become a ghostwriter – and even though you've never worked as a professional ghostwriter, you *do* have expertise in writing because you've done a lot of it in your spare time.

Your expertise is not defined by where you are in your journey or your job title. It's defined by whether you know more about a particular topic than someone else does. Or whether you know something about a topic that someone else might find interesting. Expertise doesn't have to be PhD level. It is simply about you having knowledge that others don't – knowledge that you are willing to share.

What seems boring to you is gold to someone else. Take tax returns, as an example. Filing a tax return isn't difficult – you add up what you've earned, deduct what you've spent, and work out how much you owe (I'm evidently not an accountant). All you need is a spreadsheet, a calculator, and, let's be honest, probably a glass of something stronger than coffee for moral support. But none of us want to do that, so a lot of us (me) pay an accountant to complete and file our tax returns for us.

If we were on top of everything, it probably wouldn't take us that long to complete our tax returns ourselves – and we could certainly figure it out! But we would rather pay someone with the expertise to do it for us. And trust me when I tell you, there are a lot of accountants who are certainly not experts. I'll tell you about the time my now ex-accountant 'forgot' to file my VAT return and pay my team another time.

You follow my drift, though. Expertise doesn't mean you have to be an expert, it just means you're knowledgeable and/or passionate about something that someone else doesn't have knowledge or passion for. Like taxes.

Steal my content strategy playbook: leverage your expertise

Around 70% of your content should be divided into the following areas:

- **Leveraging your experience.** Using your journey, skills and knowledge to post about things that have happened in your job role or life that provide relevant lessons or experiences for your audience.

- **FAQs.** Make a list of the questions you get asked most often in what you do and answer them in your posts. This is one of the most powerful tools for positioning yourself as an authority in your space – and someone who is willing to give away their knowledge for free.

- **Teach and tell.** Give your audience a free pass to your lived experience. Your posts have to give them more than they can find on Google by themselves. Share practical how-tos, explainers, analysis and deep dives. Give 100% of your knowledge away for free.

- **Trendspotting.** Keep your finger on the pulse of your industry and post about the latest trends and shake-ups as often as possible. This is all about leading the conversation.

Finding value in every piece of content

Everyone talks about sharing valuable content online. But what the hell is valuable content? Well, in short, it depends on the audience. I find memes valuable, for example. They're sort of my love language, actually. My point being, it doesn't have to be educational or even intelligent to be valuable. Your content could teach someone something, or make them laugh – both are valuable.

I add value by sharing my stories about building and growing my personal brand and my business – the ups, the downs, the funny-only-in-hindsight calamitous moments I've pulled myself out of. That content is valuable because it resonates with my audience: founders and executives. I also share memes. How it feels to deal with @user123456 with no profile picture telling you your content is s**t is one I like to come back to, often. I once posted, 'Building a start-up is like being waterboarded at Disney World – terrifying but fun' on LinkedIn. I received dozens of comments from other founders who just *got it*. That post was valuable to the people I'm trying to create value with, because they could see themselves in it. (And who doesn't love feeling like there's someone out there who understands them?)

Value, in monetary terms, varies from person to person. It's also determined by the person you're trying to 'sell' to. The monetary value of my expertise is $6,500 per day – to some people that might sound extraordinarily expensive. To others, $6,500 might sound really cheap because I'm probably going to teach them something that would take them years to figure out on their own. I've saved them time and energy. 'Value' is determined by your audience.

But you also need to think about value in terms other than money and transactional information. While writing this book, I had a schmoozing dinner with a client. It was a really simple meal and we spent a few hours chatting about running a business, our families, and so on. At the end of the evening he told me that our chat had been one of the best conversations he'd had in nearly two years. He's a solo founder, doesn't have a huge board and not many of his friends run businesses. He found the few hours we spent together talking about running a business incredibly valuable – and it had nothing to do with money or transactional information. It was just the power of feeling understood by another human – being a good listener is also incredibly valuable!

Once you've got a handle on what's valuable to your ideal audience, whether it's educational content and/or memes, you also have to consider what *you* value – the two are intrinsically linked. Take how people often message me saying that I've inspired them or that I've helped them become more confident. That's valuable to them, and boosting people's confidence is something *I* value too. And none of that is about my expertise, or education in a traditional sense. It's about someone feeling as though something is missing, and that I have the key to unlocking that in them. And on the flipside, it's really important to me that I inspire people to come on this journey with me – because it's changed my life. What people want from me and what I want to give to the world are one and the same.

From my content strategy playbook: getting personal

Around 30% of your content should be divided into the following areas:

- **The personal touch.** Talk about how you got to where you are and what your career journey has been. Explain why you do what you do. Share your failures, learnings and give people a window into who you are as a person. For most of us, this content will feel the most uncomfortable to post, but it will also get the most engagement.

- **Your everyday life.** Give people an insight into your day-to-day life. Don't underestimate the power of documenting your life. Remember that what's boring to you might be golden to someone else.

- **Tales of triumph.** If you've got some killer case studies or success stories up your sleeve, share them! These stories are proof that you are who your content says you are, so shout about the project you aced or the challenge you solved by turning it on its head.

Using your expertise and value to create audience resonance

OK, so by now you should be pretty blooming clear on what your 'core pillars' are – what you *do* and who you *are*, aka your expertise and your story. Let's now start thinking about how you can make both of those things resonate with your *ideal* audience. First up, what do your audience give a s**t about? Let's say your expertise is in copywriting, and what you really value is storytelling, but your audience is mainly pharmaceutical marketing managers. If you only talk about copywriting or storytelling, they will have little to no interest in your content. Their problems are less about copy, and more about helping the business win sales! However, if you share content about how pharmaceutical companies can position their product and marketing in a way that will win attention, and business. . . you see where I am going with this?

Like I said before, audience resonance is the acid test for every piece of content you produce. Remember when I told you I always say to my team when we run through client content 'what's the f**king point?' in Chapter 4? If your ideal audience can't see the point in a piece of content straight away, then they're not going to care about it. And you will have wasted your time. Everyone you're trying to appeal to needs to understand every piece of your content and what it means to *them*. They need to see the value in it immediately.

Resonating with your audience isn't only about talking about the right topics – it's talking about the right topics *in the right way*. Imagine you work for a Ferrari or Porsche dealership, you might want to talk about how the engines in the cars are built, because the people who typically buy those kinds of cars care about that stuff. However, if you want to sell an MG 4 × 4 to a mum of three, she probably doesn't give a s**t about the engine size. She probably cares about how much baggage she can fit in the boot while using every seat and whether or not the sound system is loud enough to drown out her children's cries. . . spoken from experience.

Both of these people are selling cars, but they are selling them to two very, very different people. They're going to need to make very different content to make sure it resonates with the person they're selling to. Good content acknowledges *dreams*, provides *painkillers*, triggers *nostalgia* or sells a *lifestyle* to their ideal audience. In other words – find the thing that people give a s**t about, and position your content to address those things.

Here are my content pillars and how the subcategories address my ideal audiences of founders, executives, marketers and, well, you:

1. Personal branding:

    a. How personal branding can increase your brand awareness by 561%.

    b. How to convert leads 7× more frequently by building your personal brand.

    c. How to create 162 pieces of content in one hour a week.

    d. How I've won new business by creating a podcast.

2. My story:

    a. Why I started building my personal brand and where I am now.

    b. My biggest failures as a business owner, and what I have learned from them.

    c. How sharing content about my biggest imperfections have led to my biggest wins in life and business.

    d. The reality of being a single mum of two and trying to juggle a career, a team and a company.

Helicopter out from these subtopics and you'll notice they're the same ideas I mentioned earlier in this chapter, but they're now specifically designed to tackle the dreams, pains, lifestyle ideals and experiences (nostalgia) of my ideal audiences. Founders can relate to business challenges, executives can relate to needing to close leads more frequently – and you can probably relate to being a working parent and, if not, failure is one we all can vibe with. Make sense?

How to use your content pillars to create never-ending content

Personally, my core pillar statement isn't something I share externally, but it is at the centre of the spider diagram that I use to brainstorm content ideas (Figure 6.1). From 'To be the go-to person for personal branding', I can work up loads of content formats. . .

- An example of how building my personal brand changed my life.

- How I manage to post every single day 365 days a year.

- A time when I made a massive f**k up in business and what I did next.

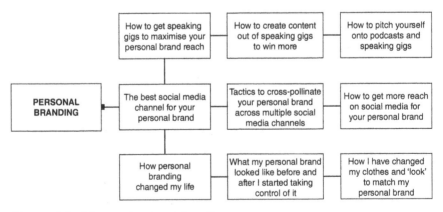

Figure 6.1: My content spider diagram.

The last point isn't to do with personal branding, but it is to do with failure – something you, my audience, can relate to. Again, your personal brand is what you *do*, but it is also who you *are*. And I am someone who goes from failure to failure without a lack of enthusiasm, which is probably why I tend to usually land on my feet. . . Don't optimise the humanity out of your personal branding content.

And – even better than that – each of those formats can be reused again and again with different examples. Below I use the same content ideas from above, but presented in a different way.

- A before and after of how building my personal brand changed my life.

- Stats from what it looks like after posting 365 days a year.

- A story about why f**king up helps you win.

I've been saying the same things over and over again for nearly six years. Once you find your content pillar(s), coming up with content ideas isn't a struggle – you just have to execute it.

Repeat your core message without becoming repetitive

I said it earlier, and I will repeat myself again. . . I have been saying the same thing, in slightly different ways for nearly six years. Not a single person has ever said to me 'you have already said that before. . .'. You can't repeat your core content pillars and message enough – you have to deliver the same message relentlessly. That's why I got to write this book, and why you're reading it. . . I am known for personal branding because I talk about it so much.

If you want to be known as *the* D2C guy, you can't only talk about D2C once a month. You have to post about it every single day. And sometimes that means repeating yourself. A lot.

Take Chris Donnelly. Founder of Verb – he wants to be known as the scale-up guy, so all he talks about is building scale-up businesses and leading teams within them. He posts a variation on the same kind of content every single day; how to scale businesses, and how to (and how not to) manage and lead people. Often he'll give the same piece of advice, but with a different example. Sometimes the same example, but just reposted with a slight variation, like the captions changed. At the time of writing, he had more than a quarter of a million followers on LinkedIn and around 15 million followers on TikTok – and all he talks about is growing businesses and leading teams.

While you have to repeat your message, be smart in how you present it. Repurpose, remix, reuse your content. If you posted something as a text post and it did well, post it as a video, or a graphic. Play around with how you presented it. Told a story? Try a one-liner and see if you get a similar response. If you're going to post like for like, I always recommend giving it a couple of months between posting – which we'll talk about in more detail in Chapter 10.

Trust me when I tell you, your audience is not going to get bored of you saying the same thing. You didn't get bored of Beckham playing football, did you? Or of Nicole Kidman acting? Everyone thinks they need to be original to be valuable. The truth is, you need to say the same thing to be valuable, that thing is why someone would follow you. Also, only around 3% of your followers will actually see each piece of content you post. On Facebook that figure is even lower – less than 0.1%. So, the idea that people care that you're sharing the same thing all the time is actually incredibly egotistical. Do not worry about it. No one cares enough about your content (or mine) to notice if what you're sharing is similar each day. They're coming to you for this information, so give it to them.

Look at Gary Vaynerchuk (Gary Vee) – he releases his *Trash Talk* videos every week and each one follows the same format. He goes to a garage sale, looks around, negotiates on the price of an item with the seller, buys the item and then sells it on eBay for a higher price. At the time of writing, he's been doing this for four years. Then you have shows like *Love Island* and *I'm A Celebrity* – they are incredibly formulaic and each year it's the same, but everyone loves them (although I'm in the camp that has never seen an episode of *Love Island*. . .).

But you get my point? Repetition makes sure that your core message gets seen and heard by more people, and the need for repetition within content creation is a conversation I have *constantly* with clients. I often laugh because I explain this concept, and the client says they understand. Four weeks later, they look at their content plan and say, 'We already said this'. Then I go through the explanation again – all of which actually demonstrates why repetition is so important. People forget, so we all need to keep sharing the same message until they remember. And then keep saying it until they *know* you for it.

Repetition pays off

When people start referring to you as an expert in your niche, you'll know the repetition is paying off. You'll start getting tagged in comments on posts where someone is looking for advice or support in that area. You'll begin getting inbound opportunities from people looking for someone with your expertise. More than that, you'll start receiving messages from people who have *never* interacted with your content before.

The growth in your following might not be as fast and furious as you dreamed of when you started this journey – whether you care to admit it or not, having 100k followers makes you feel important, but you don't need hundreds of thousands of followers to have a strong personal brand. You might have 5,000 followers, but if those 5,000 people are obsessed with your content and you get 4,000 people looking at every post you share, then you're smashing it.

One thing it's useful to remember across all social platforms, but particularly on LinkedIn, is that many people will look at content but not engage with it. So, don't get hung up on the likes or the number of followers you have – if you want to be known for your expertise in a particular area, it's far more important to look at the views you get on your posts, and most importantly who is viewing it. If you are getting interactions and views from people you want to impress, then a comment from them in-person is more valuable than 200 likes on a post.

Click moments

To build awareness of you and your personal brand, you need to make sure people know you for one thing and one thing only. Choose your core content pillar(s) or message and then put it at the heart of every piece of content you produce. Repeat it relentlessly. If you want to be famous, you have to be famous for something.

7

Content

Let me start this chapter by saying, content is everywhere. And I don't mean TikTok dance trends or viral videos of cats paw-slapping their owners. This book is content. So is the latest Netflix docuseries you're obsessed with. That podcast you listen to every week. That conversation you had with your friend last week about that topic you're so passionate about. And when you can wrap your head around that concept, you realise that creating content for your personal brand isn't actually difficult at all, because everything you need to say to attract the audience you want already exists.

When *I* think of content, I think of an exchange of knowledge. To me, it goes *way* beyond just the media I create and consume – it's *everything*. From that water cooler moment I had with my teammate; the smile I didn't get back when I walked past that stranger in the street; the meeting I had with my team about why 54% of internet users use TikTok but less than 25% post content on it. . . It's all content. And that I think is one of the biggest blockers for people in creating their own content for their personal brand – knowing what to say.

Maybe you can relate. You've dedicated 25 minutes in your diary to creating something to post online, only to get to the allotted time with nothing but fuzz between your ears. I've been there. But the reason you're stuck is because you're looking at this all wrong. I've said it before and I'll say it again, building a strong personal brand is only 10% content and 90% consistency in posting it. So once you're clear on what you want to be known for and to who (if not, why are you reading this chapter?), taking inspiration from your everyday conversations or the podcast you just listened to and sharing those thoughts online become simple.

I like to think about your personal brand like a high-interest account. The more you pay in, the more that compounds into big brand equity. So, whether you get one like on a post (from your mum) or 50 likes, 100 likes, *even 1,000 likes*, it really doesn't matter. Zoom out and look at the bigger picture. If you were paying in $1 every day for a year, you wouldn't have $365, in a high-interest account, you'd have $401.50. And the following year, even if you only continued to pay in $1, you'd have $843.15. The power of compound interest – it all starts with $1, or one like. So, stop stressing about that one post you did that got 'no engagement' and start thinking about the bigger picture that piece of content adds to. If you're posting content online, you're making an investment in your personal brand, and your future. And that investment will eventually build to something way, *way* more important than a handful of validating heart emojis from strangers – your reputation.

And, yes, this is a long game. But so is saving money. You can't buy a home with the $843.15 mentioned earlier – you have to keep adding to that high-interest account for a long time. And, of course, there are people that will tell you they can help make you go 'viral' in 90 days, and, of course, you've read about the overnight success stories. But guess what? You can't short-cut reputation-building. That is why focusing on the individual performance of your content, while informative on a granular level, cannot be the source of validation you use to prove or disprove how good your content – and your personality – really are.

If you only look at the individual performance of one piece of content and it flops (which it does, even at 150,000 followers), you will think you're doing something wrong and you'll stop actually producing content altogether. But you've not factored in the proper data before making your silly, self-deprecating assumptions. The time of day you posted, the medium you shared, the opening line, was it captioned? Did it make sense? Were you actually addressing something that your ideal audience cares about? Is the algorithm being updated on that particular day? There are so many factors as to why an individual piece of content doesn't perform – just like there are so many factors as to why an individual asset class or stock exchange doesn't perform on any given day.

Identifying why it hasn't performed is the important bit. Learn from it and apply those lessons but don't stop investing in your personal brand. You wouldn't stop putting money away for that house you wanted to buy because your high-interest account dipped in value due to a geopolitical influence on the stock market, would you? No. You'd appreciate that it is part of the long game of investing. Just like your personal brand.

Zoom out. It helps put any likes you do get, even if it's just one, in the context of building your brand equity. You're paying into *your* high-interest savings account and everything you put in counts. So whether that is one like a day, or 1,000 in two weeks' time and then another handful in a month. Paying in consistently is key – so, while the content you share is important, it's equally important to keep coming back to your broader goals and *why* you're taking control of your personal brand.

Another way I like to look at this whole idea is a bit philosophical. To me, creating content is the difference between being a consumer and being a creator. The difference between someone letting life happen to them, and someone making life happen for them. Read that sentence twice. Sharing content that is going to grow your reputation and get you into rooms you otherwise don't have access to is a way to make something happen for you; *it's taking action*. It's looking at your life and going, 'I know what I want, and I am not going to wait for someone to give it to me.' And if you allow a piece of content that got 'no engagement' to stop you from pursuing what you want, then you have bigger problems than posting content online. Put it down as part of the process, create your next piece and just f**king post it.

When you first start posting, it's really easy to look at what everyone else is doing and think it's a good idea to copy the viral formula they've discovered and apply it to your content. This is a huge mistake. There is a reason why it's called *personal* branding, and not just branding, period. You have to think a lot more holistically about what your personal brand represents – aka what you want to represent – and ensure that what you're sharing online matches that. Because if the content you're sharing online makes you out to be a helpful, happy, smiley and lovely person, but when I meet you in real life you're that person who is rude to waiters, all the momentum – and brand equity – you've built are lost.

As I said before, content is everything. It's not just a way for you to prove your worth online, it goes far beyond that. It is how you look, how you act, what you post and how you communicate with people – and you need to make sure that your content online and offline are aligned. The easiest way to do this? Just be your gorgeous self. I've already told you in Chapter 1 about constructive interference. Authenticity is the highest frequency we emit as humans – it's also the most attractive. Besides, it's much harder to pretend to be someone you're not than it is just to be who you really are.

Take the Kardashians as an example – they share their entire lives, everything from breakups and husbands cheating on them, to business challenges and even miscarriages. Is it all planned, strategic and well lit? Sure. But it is a reflection of their real lives. Now, I know a lot of people don't consider the Kardashians to be authentic, but you can't deny *just how much* they share about their lives online – *so much* that I'd argue they're more authentic than most of us when it comes to their content. You get the tears, the sister fights, the divorce drama. Because of that, I reckon it's unsurprising that they have such a large following – people are attracted to that perceived authenticity.

I don't advocate having your own reality TV show – we're not here to be famous. But we are here to be famous to the right people, and in order to get in front of *them*, your content is going to have to honestly and authentically reflect *you*.

The attraction of authenticity

I post a lot of content. At the time of writing, I get around 2.9 million impressions per month, organically. Brands pay big bucks for those kinds of eyeballs in advertising. But I've found this trend that every single time I post something I'm not that excited about, or am not that bothered about, the post tanks. Now, I know I said earlier don't worry about if your content gets no likes – that isn't the point I'm making here. If I upload something *I'm* not excited about, why the hell should *anyone else* be?

Social media and branding people always say 'create content with your audience in mind' – I also have been trying to hammer that message home for the past few chapters of this book! And while I still stand by it – you need to make sure you don't lose your *own* excitement or passion for what you're talking about *just* to please your audience. We started with your goal, to work out your audience, in order to discover what you need to be known for by them so you can build your brand to achieve your goal. Right? But don't lose sight of the bigger picture here, which is your personal brand is you and you are your personal brand. Creating something you're genuinely excited about sharing makes other people excited too. And excitement = engagement.

More than that, think about how infectious enthusiasm and excitement are in face-to-face conversations. Imagine you're in a bar and your best friend is talking about something he's really, really passionate about. As he speaks, he lights up and you can't help but be drawn in. Or that girl you met, when she talks about the thing she loves to do – how the smile creeps around her face. You can't help but smile as well. Excitement and passion are engaging and they're infectious because they're authentic – and it's the same online. People often tell me that they're drawn to my content for its honesty, but also for the fact that I seem like quite a happy and excitable person.

But being excited about your content doesn't mean that all of your content has to be positive – there are plenty of people in this world who have built very successful brands by being negative. If that's authentic to who you are, then *by all means* go in that direction. I'm not sure I'd follow someone who was miserable, but it's the authenticity of your content that will draw people in, not whether you're always happy. And maybe I'm not your target audience.

Understanding content channels

I'm hoping by now you're clear on what your core message or pillars are. So now we need to work out which channels you're going to be sharing all that amazing content on.

It is very difficult to create content if you don't understand what the right distribution channels for posting it are. I like to think of each channel like speaking a different language – I talked about this earlier in Chapter 3. If you walk into a room filled with people who all speak different languages, you won't say 'Hello', to all of them. That might be how you greet the British or Australian in the room, but you'd say, 'Bonjour', to the French person, 'Hola', to the Spanish person, and so on. Your message to everyone there is the same, but your delivery changes.

It's no different when it comes to using different social media channels for sharing your content. No matter which channel you're posting on, your message should stay the same. What does change, however, is the medium or context you deliver that message in.

Let's say your core message or pillar is about how to build a personal brand on LinkedIn. You might write a written post to share on LinkedIn – you know, a sort of micro blog with a picture. But you could then take that post, read it out as a script and turn it into a short video to share on TikTok. You're delivering the same message in a way that's contextualised for each of those platforms – and understanding how to distribute your content in a way that each platform understands is key to succeeding when it comes to growing your personal brand.

I get asked a lot, 'Which is the best channel to grow my personal brand?' The answer is whatever channel your audience is on. If your customers are executives of big companies, there is no point spending all your time and energy posting on TikTok, you need to go to LinkedIn.

When you're starting out on your personal brand journey, my advice is not to build on every channel from the beginning – who has time or the headspace for that? As I said earlier, I built up my personal brand on LinkedIn for the best part of two-and-a-half years before even attempting any other channels, because that's where my main audience – B2B founders, executives and entrepreneurs – were spending most of their time. I was blinkered and focused with my efforts. And, *only once* my profile was growing naturally on LinkedIn did I expand my activities to other platforms, starting with Instagram, then TikTok, then YouTube. Think of these platforms like a pyramid, with the most important one for your audience at the top. Once you're flying there, you add the next layer down.

How to create content with Klowt

#1 Know your core pillars

Most of the people I've spoken to on the Get Klowt platform tell me that the number one thing they struggle with when it comes to developing their personal brand is knowing what to say. This is why I took you through an exercise in Chapter 6 to help you gain clarity over your core message. When *you know* what you want to be *known for*, creating content is a lot easier.

#2 Give your knowledge away for free

As I said in Chapter 6, most people want to be known as an expert in something – in order to be seen as an expert, you have to give 100% of your knowledge *away for free*. It might sound counterintuitive – but *do not* gatekeep your knowledge. Because people's attention is far more valuable than a quick pay cheque. Focus on sharing your knowledge for free to build credibility and trustworthiness. Both of those things will pay you 1000 × more in the future than what you'd get for charging for your knowledge now.

Too many people fall into the trap of believing that if they charge money for something, they shouldn't give that same information out on social media. *Don't be one of those people* – because giving your knowledge away freely actually has the opposite effect. Before people will be prepared to part with their cash for your expertise, they need to see what you're offering as valuable. The best way to get them to that point is to literally show them the value you can offer. They need to know that you're the right person for the job. That means what you're saying on your social media channels *has* to be valuable enough that someone would be *prepared to pay for it*. When you give all of your knowledge away for free, you're positioning yourself as someone who knows what they're talking about, who's an authority in their space and who is generous with their knowledge. This builds credibility and trust – with that come referrals, and those referrals will ultimately make you more money. And those people who are paying you will refer you to more people who will pay you. I told you, your knowledge will produce a 1000 × bigger return on investment than asking for their credit card now. Trust me, I've been giving my knowledge away for free for years now and have generated, at the time of writing, $4 million off the back of it.

Remember that people are lazy. It's not personal. We just like easy. So, *even* if you give away everything someone needs to be able to do what you do for a living, for themselves (which I regularly do), 99% won't take the action required. Instead, they will pay *you* to do it for them.

#3 Valuable content comes in many forms

Remember how I said that not all valuable content will be educational or intelligent – that funny content can be *just* as valuable? Well, while I was writing this book, I received an inquiry at Klowt from someone who wanted to build their brand as a thought leader. He said he wanted us to create a 'profound' piece of content every day. I asked why he felt he needed that, and his reply was, 'Because I'm trying to be a thought leader.'

I challenged him, asking, 'Why does every post need to be profound? Do you have a profound thought every single day?' He told me he didn't.

And, of course, he didn't, we all have days where we're more focused on making our kids laugh or remembering to file our tax returns, or working out what to cook for dinner. Most days, in fact. When was the last time you had a profound thought? Not often. Not for me anyway. So how could he expect his content to be an authentic representation of him if he only wanted to post profound thoughts? More than that, he had made the mistake of thinking that thought leaders need to say things that are original and groundbreaking and *nothing else*. How unrelatable. . .

The reality is that most of the world's biggest thought leaders that this guy wanted to emulate state the obvious – and that is why they're thought leaders.

Look at Simon Sinek, Steven Bartlett, or Ryan Holiday – all of them state the obvious, but they do it in a way that *everyone* can understand and resonate with – a way that makes you go, 'That's me!' They make complex, human experiences and ideas simple. I do it too. My message is relatively clear: build your personal brand. I share stuff that you relate to – it's why you're reading this book.

Take Klowt's client John (not his real name), the CEO of a large cybersecurity firm. His main audience is developers, who are notoriously difficult to reach online because they don't tend to be that active on social media. If we went with the theory like the previously mentioned client had, which was all content needed to be profound, not only would we get zero engagement from them, we'd probably alienate them. In my experience, developers aren't a fan of people with an overinflated sense of self. So, how did we get around this? We created a load of memes around problems developers face, and John shared them on Reddit, X (formerly Twitter), and LinkedIn. The engagement John got was great because developers thought the memes were hilarious – because they were inspired directly by the things they were complaining and making jokes about in their favourite forums. The result? Developers wanted to follow John because he was stating the obvious. He was producing content they could relate to and see themselves in. Simple, really.

The point is, your content doesn't need to look like you have a PhD to be perceived as valuable. Just look at how many followers meme accounts have for evidence of that.

#4 Write your posts for 12-year-olds

Simplicity sells, complexity doesn't. It doesn't matter whether your audience do have PhDs, your content has to be simple, otherwise no one will want to read it. My advice is always to speak and write as though you are speaking or writing to a 12-year-old. This is around a grade 6 or grade 7 reading level. Because it doesn't matter how smart your audience is, people want the information they need or want delivered in a simple way. It's why Elon Musk is the most famous entrepreneur in the realm of new technology, because he has worked out how to communicate very complex ideas in a very simple way – both online and off. One of my favourite tweets of his was a poll he did about tunnels. Google it.

And if you struggle to get your point across in 120 characters or less, Coco Chanel once said: 'Before you leave the house, look in the mirror and take one thing off.'[1] Apply this tactic to every piece of content you share. Read it out loud and ask yourself, is this as simple as this could be? If you see or hear something that feels like fluff or unnecessary complexity, remove it.

This rule applies no matter what medium your content is in, or how long it is. Whether you're writing a short post for X, a 1,500-word blog for LinkedIn or creating a video for TikTok, always keep your content simple and easy to understand.

#5 Get to the point

It takes just two seconds for someone to decide whether to give you their attention or not. Probably less on TikTok. So, it doesn't matter if you're writing a blog post or making a video or giving a speech – you need to get the point as quickly as possible or you risk losing your audience.

You do not need to give your life story, or consider every person's perspective in a single piece of content. That's what the comments section is for.

I like to start thinking about my posts from the point I want to make, and work backwards from there – finding a story or analogy to support them. That helps me avoid a mistake I see loads on social media: people share what they *think* is an 'interesting story', but too often there is no point to it. Remember to always ask 'what's the f**king point?' with a capital F.

Here's an example of how I apply this in a piece of content. The point I want to make is that you need to post consistently on social media to build a brand. Even though it's simple, I can't just say, 'You have to post all the time if you want to build a personal brand on social media' because that's not engaging, it's a little too obvious and it won't be perceived as valuable enough by my audience for them to sit up and listen. Or engage.

So, instead, I might tell a story about how I wanted to lose some weight, so I started going to the gym. After three weeks I gave up, and then was surprised I hadn't lost the weight. When I realised that a lack of consistency was the reason I hadn't lost the weight, I restarted at the gym and over the course of five more weeks, I started achieving the weight loss I wanted. Then I can tie that back into how if you don't post consistently, you won't see the results you want for your personal brand. That resonates way more, right?

Every post you put out into the world should have a key takeaway. Now, you don't have to explicitly state, 'So the key takeaway from this is . . .' but everyone reading your post should leave with one, high-impact thing that is blindingly obvious because you've articulated your point in a way that is easy for your audience to understand. Even if that high-impact thing is a giggle because the meme you shared is so damn relatable.

#6 Use calls to conversation, not calls to action

'Like this post for a discount!' 'DM me for more information!' No one wants to feel like they're being sold to – and yet you continue to put these nonsense sentences at the bottom of your posts. So, skip them in favour of what I think of as 'calls to conversation'. Encourage people to have a conversation with you about what you've just posted. You'll get much more engagement.

Personal branding isn't about sales, it's about positioning yourself as an expert in your space and generating top-of-funnel brand awareness. If you do this well, and your content resonates with the right people, the sales will come – often without you even having to ask for them. Even if people in your audience don't buy from you directly, they will refer you to others who do.

Gary Vee has a book called *Jab, Jab, Jab, Right Hook*, where he talks about how you should have three pieces of valuable content for every piece of sales content.[2] I actually think you need to share 13 pieces of valuable content – where you give your knowledge away for free – before you ask for anything. And I mean *anything*! Then do it all again.

The top-line goal you have for growing your personal brand might be to generate more leads, but the outcome for each piece of content should be to get people talking in the comments – that's what's going to drive more eyeballs to your content and *that's* how you'll generate more leads in the long term. Personal branding isn't about advertising or sales, it's about your reputation. You can't ask for anything in return when you're building a brand. Give your knowledge away for free.

You need to see every post you make like a mini keynote – you wouldn't walk around with a hat and ask people for money at the end of a keynote, would you? But you might invite people to come and speak to you after your talk, which will likely result in a deeper connection, conversation, and business further down the line.

Practice makes perfect

While I wish there was a cheat code, the only way you'll ever get better at articulating your point and explaining complex ideas simply is through practice. You have to start producing content, put it out there and monitor how it performs.

Don't be afraid of some posts performing better or worse than others. Instead, be willing to learn what you could have done better with each one. So, if you share a post on LinkedIn and only get 10 likes, when usually you get 50, look at that underperforming post to see what you did differently. Perhaps there was an extra paragraph at the beginning that didn't need to be there. Maybe you over- or under-explained something. Or you used too much jargon. The more you analyse the posts that performed poorly as well as those that performed well, the more consistently good your content creation will become.

A quick note on jargon – sometimes people fall into the trap of thinking it's OK to use industry jargon in their content, because their audience will understand it. But even if people know what the jargon means, they still want simplicity. Remember what I said about writing for a 12-year-old and using language that *everyone* can understand? Don't forget it.

Also, I know this question is coming, so I may as well anticipate it now. Don't get hung up on what time of day you're posting content on social media. If your message is strong enough, it will get picked up, regardless of whether it drops at 3 p.m. on a Tuesday or 9 p.m. on a Sunday. Sharing content regularly is the most important thing. *Do* first, *optimise* later.

Identifying your tone of voice

Tone of voice is a tricky thing, because you need to be an amplified, often more direct version of how you communicate in real life. I, for one, am very direct in my language online but in person don't shut up. So, the best way to work out how your voice needs to come across online is to look at table 7.1 and work out which of these 12 celebrities you most identify with. Have a go now.

Whichever of those people you most identify with, go away and watch some videos of them speaking. Find some of their written content and read it. This will give you a really good starting point for developing your own tone of voice and help you define how you want to communicate online.

Table 7.1: Celebrities and their particular style

Mentor	Tony Robbins: his content makes you feel as though he wants to help you find your way
Charming	Justin Trudeau: he's incredibly charming when he speaks, which is why people like him
Bold	Gary Vee: he's direct, gets straight to the point and is happy being assertive
Commander	Winston Churchill: he commands attention and forces people to listen to him
Crusader	Malcolm X: he inspires people through a journey that you're all going on together
Storyteller	Steve Jobs: he leveraged analogies and everyday human experiences to inspire people to buy Apple products
No bulls**t	David Goggins: he doesn't care what people think and cuts the crap
Inspirational	Oprah: she tells other people's inspirational stories to get her point across
Philosophical	Jordan Peterson: he introduces complex ideas but communicates them in a simple and direct way
Empathetic	Jacinda Ardern: she uses empathy for her audience's situations and challenges to land her point
Sales person	Warren Buffet: everything he says is a sales play, you buy into him all the time
Technical	Elon Musk: he explains things simply, but in often very granular detail. Just seek out his speaking gigs online.

Once you've done that little exercise, it's also useful to look back over content you've already created and view it through the lens of that tone of voice. So, if you really want to come across as a mentor, like Tony Robbins, have you truly coached others in your previous posts? You have to challenge yourself and understand that if you want to be perceived as that kind of person, you need to evaluate your content to make sure it hits the right tone. Go do that *now*.

Talk like you've had an espresso

When you're creating any kind of content – whether video, audio or written – you need to take your enthusiasm and excitement up a level. This is something I talk about a lot with other people who've built strong brands online. I think there's a mistake people make in associating the word 'authentic' with 'talk like you do with your friends'. If, when you're delivering your TikTok or keynote you think you're being over the top, you're probably in the right place – this is what will allow your personality to come through. If you just read a script in a normal, monotone voice, you will come across as flat and, most likely, a bit dull. Not things one would normally associate with 'virality'.

So act like you've had an espresso. Perk up. Be expressive. Use your hands if you want to – show you care. When you demonstrate that you're amped up and excited, other people get excited too. When you're producing content, it's very difficult to get that excitement and personality across unless you slightly dial up your personality. Remember, you want to stand *out*, not blend *in*.

This isn't inauthentic – you're still being yourself, you're just being yourself on your best day. But if you can't do that, you won't cut through the noise.

Sell with emotion, back it up with facts

The difference between telling a story and being a great storyteller is the emotion you manage to trigger in the person you're telling the story to. Steve Jobs was a great storyteller – it was what helped him grow Apple to the huge success it is. One of the best examples of his storytelling ability came when Apple launched the iPod.

Steve Jobs could have stood on stage and said, 'This is a 10 GB MP3 player that you can carry in your pocket instead of having a portable CD player.' Factually, that would all have been true. But I personally would have switched off at 10 GB.

What he actually said was, 'With iPod, Apple has invented a whole new category of digital music player that lets you put your entire music collection in your pocket and listen to it wherever you go. With iPod, listening to music will never be the same again.'[3]

With his storytelling, Steve Jobs sold the lifestyle, the dream, and the intangible emotional side of the products Apple launched. He put our hearts, our souls, our nostalgia and our happiest, and saddest, memories into our pockets. He never focused on the technical features – he focused on what the technology would bring to people's lives. And that is why Apple sold 450 million iPods.

Steve Jobs' storytelling might have centred around Apple's products, but the same principles apply when you're being a storyteller for your personal brand. Focus on the emotions, not just on the facts. If I told people that I've got 150,000 followers on LinkedIn and I'm great at personal branding and this is what they should do. . . No one would listen to me.

Instead I tell people about my journey from zero to 150,000 LinkedIn followers. I talk about how hard it's been to get to this point, and

I share things that I've learned on my journey that might help others. I talk about the fact that building my personal brand has allowed me to leave an unfulfilling marriage, own my own home, fly around the world doing something I love and get paid to do it. I talk about how personal branding has changed my life. With passion and with emotion. Remember what I said about selling lifestyles, painkillers and dreams? I back up my stories with education and facts, but 70% of a buying decision – whether true purchase or 'follow' button click – is made with emotion. You have to trigger those in people if you want them to listen to what you have to say.

Follow the engagement loop

There are three aspects to the engagement loop in this context. The first is the feedback you get from your followers. What questions do they ask in the comments section? Is there anything they want to hear more or less about? The comment section is a goldmine, because you can take what people are saying and turn that into future pieces of content.

The second aspect of the engagement loop means having the humility and self-awareness to look at the content you're sharing and challenge yourself to improve it. As much as I talk about not giving a s**t about the number of followers and likes you have (to be clear, I still don't), you do need to regularly assess your content to make sure it's resonating with your audience *and* that you are getting engagement from those people. Otherwise, what is the point?

If it's not resonating, just tweak it and put it back out there. Rinse and repeat until you start seeing engagement from the *right people* – which is the real sign that what you're saying resonates with your audience. Don't only do this with your underperforming content – this works for content that does well too.

At Klowt we call this process 'skyscrapering'. If a piece of content goes viral, we'll keep reposting it, remixing it and repurposing it until it stops doing well. The point is, a high-performing piece of content can gather momentum and climb the metaphorical skyscraper if it's reshared enough. This is a really great way to squeeze maximum juice from your content. Remember what I said in Chapter 6 about repeating your message? Not everyone will see everything you post the first time around. Besides, not repurposing your content is like only wearing a great outfit once. Dumb and expensive.

Point three of the engagement loop – what if you are stuck for content ideas? Just speak to your ideal audience or your clients and ask them what they care about. The feedback you gather from those conversations will help you create a content plan that resonates with people just like them. That *they* want to *engage* with. It's really not that hard.

The engagement loop simply means you're listening to your audience and understanding their response to you and what you're saying – those could be comments and shares or they could be emails and phone calls and actual real-life conversations. Your ideal audience needs to inform what you talk about – if they're not engaging with what you're sharing, that's feedback in itself. It's your job to work out why.

Some of the most common reasons why your content may not be getting the engagement you're looking for are:

- Your posts are too complicated.

- You're trying to say too many things at once.

- You're using passive language. Boring.

- You're speaking to the universal audience as opposed to the individual – don't ask what your 'followers' think about something, ask people what '*you*' think about something. People identify as people, not as followers.

- You think you need to talk about everything – you don't, you just need to be an expert in one thing. Don't dilute your message.

- You don't know who your audience is – if you're still saying that your audience is B2B businesses, for goodness sake, re-read Chapter 5!

Click moments

When you understand that content is way more than just what you post on social media, it opens up your eyes to where and how you can actually be positioning yourself as a person of influence. Following the six rules for creating content with Klowt will help you to stay on message, on brand and on track to building a f**king great personal brand with the people you want to create it with.

8

Creating your visual brand

I remember going into one of my first big pitch meetings. I felt confident. I know my stuff. I was wearing sneakers, black leggings and my Klowt-branded hoodie. I was representing my company – no one was ever going to doubt what business I had come from. I delivered my pitch – nailed it (or so I thought).

As we got to the end of the meeting, I was asked a few questions, I reiterated a few points, shook the prospective clients' hands and walked out. It had gone well. I'd made a good impression. As I walked out of the room and turned left down the corridor towards reception I walked past one of our competitors. He was obviously there to pitch for the same business. We made the briefest eye contact and shared a smile.

He was wearing black trousers, sneakers and a company-branded hoodie.

Your personal brand isn't just what you post online – it's what you wear, how you act. It can be easy to forget that your personal brand isn't just about your ideas and knowledge. Your personal brand is external too. And I get it, you're going to read this and say, 'You shouldn't judge a book by its cover', well, life isn't fair. And people do judge you on how you show up – mentally and physically. When I walked past my competitor after that pitch meeting, my visible personal brand was screaming 'same'. We looked identical, and aside from our company-branded hoodies, there was nothing visually separating us. The opposite of what personal branding is all about.

I couldn't stop thinking about it all the way back to the office. I'm the person who talks about standing out being your superpower – and here I was, dressed exactly the same as a guy looking to win the same business as me. I always say, 'Don't be vanilla', and yet I looked like I was the same flavour as the other guy. That was the moment I decided to change my visual brand.

At the beginning of 2023, I completely rebranded myself aesthetically. I dyed my hair to the signature blonde I have now, I worked with a stylist to overhaul my wardrobe and find my 'look'. I made a conscious effort to blow my hair out, find my signature make-up look – I completely took control of how I showed up, externally. I decided pink was my colour, even though it's not something I would typically have chosen to wear. And I took control of how people perceived me at first impression.

And, look, I am not going to ditch my hoodies and leggings completely. I love them. And on the days that I work from home, it makes sense to be comfortable – and still represent the business on Zoom calls. However, I love dressing up. I love wearing suits and dresses and heels or trainers. I love having my hair done, my make-up on point – I love my distinctively long blonde hair. I love to look like I've got my s**t together, because that is what makes me feel powerful.

And when you look like you've got your s**t together, people normally think you do. And people want to do business with people who have their s**t together. Before my brand screamed 'same', now it stands confidently in 'different'. How I look sets the tone for what my personal brand stands for, and so should yours.

That's not to say you need to wear a suit or throw on a pair of heels (whatever floats your boat. . .). My point isn't about damaging your feet; my point is about how you dress and how people perceive you – and how people perceive you determines how valuable you become. So, why try to give yourself a disadvantage, because you want to be comfy? Why try and fight against a system because you want to have a reason to wear a pair of tracksuit bottoms to work? Stop devaluing yourself. Stop intentionally blending in like I was because you don't think it's fair that people judge your abilities in part on how you present yourself. If you hate wearing suits, don't wear a suit – it's inauthentic and you'll come across awkward! All I'm saying is there are so many ways to get a head start in life, but one of the easiest ones is to look the part.

So, make an effort – it will get you everywhere.

Building your authentic visual brand

For some people, 'looking the part' comes naturally to them. I am not one of those people. And if you're like me and are far more at home in activewear and joggers than you are in a suit, we need to get serious about how you're showing up visually with your personal brand. Perception is important. You really do only get one shot to make a good first impression, let's make sure it counts.

What is *your* 'style'?

- What do you feel most confident in? Seems simple enough but wearing what makes you feel good is often the key to a great visual personal brand.

- Think about your favourite clothes. What do they have in common and why? For example, are they all black because that's attuned to your personality? Or are they all brightly coloured because your energy is too?

- What pieces do I wear all the time?

- What do I want my personal style to say about me before I've even opened my mouth?

To be honest, there is a balance to be found here. It's kind of half authenticity – I'd never want you to wear something that didn't feel aligned to who you are – and half controlling how others perceive you. How do you want to show up in that room, and what can you wear to ensure that happens? And, by the way, what I'm talking about isn't dressing in the way your audience *expects* you to. I have a good friend who is the Managing Partner of a VC and only wears hoodies – it's about dressing in a way that visually shows off your identity, and projects to your audience a narrative that you've crafted about who you are. It's a subtle difference, but an important one.

Think about Steve Jobs. He was an innovator, and when all the tech CEOs around him were wearing suits, he wore Levi's, New Balance and black turtlenecks. And he wore Levi's, New Balance and black turtlenecks from the early 1990s all the way through to his death in 2011. It became his brand. Being is the operative word, because no one other than Steve Jobs dressed like that. It set the tone for who he was, but also for Apple. It screamed simplicity but also challenging the status quo – something that later became an Apple motto.

Jobs always maintained he dressed like a Bond villain because he didn't want to have to worry about what to wear every day, but I think it was much more strategic than that. The fact that we're still talking about how he dressed now shows you how effective his visual brand was.

And Steve Jobs is just one small example. Look at Marilyn Monroe's bleached blonde hair and red lips, or Will.I.Am's glasses, or Pharrell Williams' hats. Even Donald Trump's fake tan, blue suit, red tie and Make America Great Again hat. There are plenty of talented, beautiful actresses, amazing musicians, and opinionated politicians – but most are just a by-line in a Sunday morning paper. The thing that Marilyn Monroe, Will.I.Am, Pharrell Williams, Donald Trump and Steve Jobs all understood is that if you want to win, you need attention. And to get attention, you have to stand out. They understood that your personal brand is external too. And that is why they're so famous.

So, instead of thinking 'what would my audience want to see?' think about how you want them to see *you*. As Henry Ford allegedly once said, 'If I had asked my customers what they wanted, they would have said faster horses.'

Strategically aligning your style to your brand

Hopefully you answered the questions I asked you in the previous section, if you haven't – go and do that now because the next thing I want you to do after you've worked out what you actually enjoy wearing, is discover how you can align that to how you want people to perceive you and your personal brand both online and off.

Go jump on Google, scroll through Instagram – I give you permission to doom scroll TikTok in search of inspiration. But what we need from this exercise is to work out who inspires you, who aligns most to your journey and authentic self, and find ways to learn how they've built their visual identity and take inspiration from them to build your own. The following questions will help.

- Whose style do you like and why?

- Whose content do you like and why?

- What brands do you like and why?

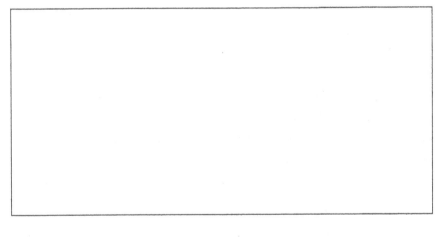

If you want to be extra strategic (always), you can take the answers to the 'why' part of those questions and translate it into a really clear visual identity. So, I'm low key obsessed with Olivia Attwood's style. If you don't know who she is, Google her. Her aesthetic perfectly matches the seriousness of her work, and the playful silliness of her personality. She presents very hard-hitting documentary series, and is also a total goofball on social media. And so, she pairs a polished 'rich girl' aesthetic with messy buns and sneakers, depending on her mood – and the platform. The perfect alignment to an authentic visual identity and brand. I've taken inspiration from her and applied it to my own personal brand.

Or maybe you say, 'I like Alex Hormozi's content because it's super direct, really impactful and I feel like I know him because of how he addresses me.' In that case, you might decide to film your video content in a tight frame, speaking directly to the camera, because that will have the same impact on the people who will engage with your content as Alex's content has had on you.

You get where I am going with this? It's not just about style – it's about how you deliver your message, how you behave in front of people. Ultimately, it's how you define who you are before you've even met someone. Which is so much more than just whether or not you wear suits or sneakers.

The evolution of your personal brand

If you're at the stage of building your personal brand where you're ready to start treating it like a business, you need to define what that brand actually looks like beyond just your style and content. Pull together a set of brand guidelines, which will span not only your personal appearance but all the visuals associated with your personal brand, from the fonts you use (I love **Bebas Neue**) to the colours. My 'colour' is pink. Obviously.

Post mortem all your decisions against how you want to be perceived, aka, if you want to be perceived as 'premium' but you're using the font Comic Sans, you've made a boo boo.

One of the things we do for clients at Klowt is define a clear visual identity mood board when we onboard them. We collect examples of videos and images that show what we're aiming for – we find inspiration in other people's content and style, because then it becomes much easier to define what a personal brand should look like if you have something to benchmark it against.

And, by the way – you don't need to do this. I didn't have a personal brand 'identity' or guidelines until 2023. And I didn't even have a website for my business until 2021. You don't need this stuff to start, so don't use it as an excuse not to.

And, equally, don't fall into the trap of thinking that you have to stick to your 'identity' once you've defined it. You're a human being who is ever-evolving – your brand should too.

Don't get stuck in a rut

Do you know what the definition of madness is? Doing the same thing over and over again and expecting a different outcome. You're a human being, you change, you evolve. Don't tie yourself down to one 'style' or clothing, visual identity or content if it no longer works for you. If I had done this, I would still have mousy brown hair and be talking about recruitment – and I'd have no business. Psychologically speaking, this is known as loss aversion, where we are more scared of potential losses than excited about potential gains. It's like when gamblers keep betting in casinos when they're on a losing streak, hoping that something will change. And why many people stay in unhappy relationships because they have invested so much time in them. *And* why you might be tempted to stick with your current style, or content – or even life. You're scared of what comes next. The mediocrity of what you're living in now is more comfortable than daring to change it.

When I changed my 'brand' – I dyed my hair, found a new way to do my make-up, changed my clothes – it helped me grow my personal brand even more. I have had at least three different careers since I took control of my personal brand, and I've never had people unfollow me because I am doing something different, have changed my appearance, or changed the content I am posting. *Never.* In fact, the opposite happens. People are interested in what's going on and why I've made a change, and I attract new people into my circle. That is the power of a personal brand. It evolves as you do.

I've said it before, and I will say it again – your personal brand is like a high-interest bank account. You wouldn't think twice about switching your account from one bank to another to get a better rate elsewhere, would you? When you change your personal style, or the content you're posting, you're just taking what you've paid into your personal branding account and moving it to where you'll get a better return.

To build an authentic personal brand is to *own* your evolution. Evolution is a natural part of life. It's not only important to evolve your brand so that it remains authentic to who you are as a person, but also because it re-engages your audience – introducing new people to who you are and what you do. Why do you think consumer brands evolve and change their identities so frequently, or football teams change their kits every year? It gives people a reason to follow your journey and fall in love with you again.

When there's no innovation, brands plateau and stagnate. Take Pizza Hut as an example – they've failed to really innovate and move beyond the 'pizza and buffet' concept we all loved as a kid. And, yeah, they deliver now – but so does everyone else. It's not really an evolution, is it? The result? They aren't adding to their customer base – and their annual revenue was 51% lower last year than it was in 2012.[1] (Even if many of us *are* nostalgic about their Ice Cream Factory.)

Who has evolved well? Formula One. Now, I'm a huge F1 fan – I grew up on a diet of Sunday roasts and Lewis Hamilton – and I think the brand is such a good example that everyone – personal and consumer brands – can follow. F1 has gone from being an old, rich, white male-only sport to capturing one of the youngest, most diverse fanbases in the world. How? *Formula One: Drive to Survive.*

Liberty Media bought Formula One from Bernie Ecclestone in 2017 and they knew that if they didn't attract a new audience, the sport would die. Who was going to sponsor an outrageously expensive motor race with no fans? *Drive to Survive* has not only introduced F1 to a whole new – much younger – audience, but it's also made everyone who's watched it buy into the teams, the engineers, the drivers (and the drama). At the time of writing, F1 has experienced incredible growth among female and young audiences.[2]

It has pivoted from being perceived as elitist and inaccessible to being one of the biggest and most-watched sports on TV. There are two clear lessons here – evolve your brand with your growth and your audience, and build your personal brand. Had to get that one in there, because let's be real; the real stars of F1 are the drivers.

So, yeah, to anyone that tells you, 'you've changed' – f**k them. Of course, you have. You didn't work this hard not to. If you're someone who wants better from their life, you need to change. Because there is nothing worse than staying the same. Both in your career, personal life, and your personal brand.

Click moments

You have to take control of other people's perceptions of you from the first moment they see you, and that means you can't turn up online or off looking like a trash raccoon. Does your personal style and visual identity align with how you want to be perceived? If not, change it. Now.

Your personal brand isn't just what you post online, it's how you look, how you dress, how you behave – it's your shop window. And that shop window needs to grow and evolve as the seasons of your life and career do.

9

Building a community, not a following

A lot of people confuse building a *community* with having a *following*. Let me tell you something – they're not the same thing. Sure, both are measured on numbers of people. Both might like your content, but there's a big difference. A following is a group of people you talk *at* – like when you give a speech or presentation. A community is a group of people who you want to talk *with*, where both you and they are interested in what the other has to say. It's about influencing people from within the group, not shouting at them from above it.

In the digital age where our entire lives are on and dictated by the internet, anyone can build a community – and almost instantly. One of the reasons why I love social media so much is because you really only need two things to build a community of people who will not only listen to what you have to say, but advocate for you too.

1. A common interest.

2. A common platform.

So for you, this could be:

1. You want to build your personal brand.

2. You enjoy reading. Hence *this* book.

And the best part? There is already a community of people that exist online that want to hear from *you*. You don't even need to work that hard to find them – you just have to say the right thing, on the right platform.

'Community' as a concept isn't new. Think about your neighbours, or your friends – you're a form of community. You all share common interests and have a common platform. But marketers have now hijacked the term to mean 'people that like us so much they will buy our s**t'. Historically, marketing used to be such a one-way street. It would be advertisers shouting at their customers, not talking with them. That changed with the introduction of social media, because customers now expect a back and forth. They want a dialogue. They want to feel seen, heard and understood. And the way you do that? Create resonance. And if you're rolling your eyes thinking, but she's said that already – get a grip. Resonance is so important, and I will continue to mention it probably eight more times in this book, because when you create resonance, when you tell stories, you make people see themselves in your content and your journey. When people see themselves in your content and your journey, they fall in love with you. They want to be a part of your community because they feel seen, heard and understood. And that is what makes you stand out from everyone else in your space, and that is what builds a strong personal brand. It's this resonance that builds a community of like-minded people – the basis of a strong personal brand. Great success.

I'm not sure I really 'got' resonance as the secret sauce of personal branding until I was so immersed in building mine that it was hard to ignore the patterns. The stories I shared with people, the networking and speaking events I've done, the Direct Messages I've had and replied to, the comments I get. There are thousands of people that talk about personal branding – the information we share as individuals on the topic isn't really unique. But the one thing that makes me stand out – and the thing that makes you stand out in your niche – is that it's *my information.* It's *my* story, *my* journey. My unique way of sharing my insights. And it's through the 'why' that people find themselves drawn to my content, because they see themselves in it. It's why I talk so much about failure, and overcoming obstacles, building resilience – even getting divorced and being fired! We all have our own version of those stories, and by sharing them as a vehicle to spread my message, I am creating resonance with people who've experienced the same thing, and thus loyalty. That's what a community is – people who will support, advocate for and refer you to others. Hopefully, you're part of mine!

The goal of building your personal brand shouldn't be to have 100,000 followers. It should be to become the most referred person in your industry. And that is what your community, when nurtured properly, will do for you. Superfans will refer you time and time again to their followers, their friends and their network and are often a much more powerful advocate than a one-off customer who you did a good job for. But, in all honesty, people will only become your advocates if you build personal relationships with them. And that is what building your personal brand does – at scale. You're able to do this on an infinite level, rather than on a one-to-one basis. Your superfans will advocate for you to an infinite number of potential customers. Find something that your tribe relates to, then continually pull that lever until they love you. Benefit from their reach as well as yours. It's the hack to business and career growth.

And let me tell you, once that momentum gets going, it's a bit like ethical network marketing, but your advocates provide free, organic, non-paid referrals back to you – and what you're selling. Whether it's a product, services, or you as an employee. And who doesn't want that? If you are able to distribute your knowledge and services through those people, you will influence a significantly larger number of potential customers than if you just sold to those individuals yourself. The result? Less work, more reward.

But, of course, this all starts with the *right* community – and knowing who you want to attract comes from knowing what your goals are. As I said earlier, my goal is to help a million people build their personal brands and be 100% OK with the consequences of being themselves. So, all of the content I share and the way I interact with people online and in-person relates directly to that goal. *But* I don't just want an audience, I want fans who are part of a community. I want people to like *me*, rather than people to like the fact I talk about personal branding. This is why I have a weekly vlog on YouTube. It's why I make dorky videos on Instagram. It's why I post what I am cooking for dinner on my stories, and why I regularly do 'ask me anything' live Q&As with actual community members.

I even have the Get Klowt membership – a paid-for community that allows people to talk directly with me. I have people in my network, whom I have never met, but who will continually refer work to me. They trust me enough to be confident in bigging me up in rooms I don't have access to, which is why Klowt is a 100% inbound business.

And, look, I am not saying you need to share your life online – if you are just aiming to be seen as a thought leader in a specific niche, you can, of course, just talk about *that* topic. But the key is to talk about it from *your* personal experience. You can't just share information and expect people to love you – if it was information people wanted, they could just go to Google. No, people want *your* information. They want to know why you have the knowledge, how you got that insight – *your* story. Your human story creates resonance that gives a reason to listen to and follow you. And that is what gives *you* a competitive advantage.

Start small

I was interviewing someone for the *Branded By Amelia Sordell* podcast the other day, and they said something along the lines of, 'Oh, I only have 5,000 followers.' *Only* 5,000 followers. I stopped them and said, 'Only? Imagine if 5,000 people were in this room right now, waiting to hear what you had to say.' He laughed. You don't need thousands of people to have a community – you could have five people. All you need to have is, as I said before:

1. A common interest.

2. A common platform.

Heck, your common interest could be hockey, or football. Or the fact that you think tea is better than coffee (it is not). You can create a community with 100 people. And if you can build a community with 100 people, I promise you those 100 people will advocate for you to other people that might like your weird tea vs. coffee content, too.

It's the same principle that underpins how bands build fanbases – a small number of people like a band initially and they introduce it to their friends, sharing their excitement and how the band inspires them. The result? Their friends get excited too, so they share the music with even more people. The Sidemen are an incredible example of this. What started off as a group of friends sharing videos of them gaming online together, has turned into a nearly $60 million business. Why? Because they found their tribe – people who loved gaming, and loved watching them game. They expanded their audience through that initial community to what it is today. Now, every single product, brand or business The Sidemen launch sells out immediately. Not bad for a bunch of friends who met playing FIFA.

When you have people who passionately believe in you and your message and support you in the pursuit of sharing it, you don't need lots of them. They will draw more people into your community and help you build it. Your only real job is to create those initial superfans.

A word of warning, there is no such thing as an overnight success. Advocacy – and building community – take time. Think of it like dating – you wouldn't get married on the second date, would you? It takes time to get to know someone and trust them enough to even want to be in a couple. Then it's more getting to know them and trust-building before you even think about 'committing'. Take the same approach to building your community. You've got to take people to dinner a few times before you start propositioning them.

So, drip-feed your knowledge and personality into it. Gradually peel back the layers of yourself, your knowledge and your skills until the community that follows you gets access to its centre. Be you, share you. That's how you create resonance, and that's how you build connections and relationships, at scale. It's only once your relationship gets that deep that they will be superfans – and, more importantly, advocates who sell for you – but don't rush this process.

Emotion before logic

You might already know this – I can certainly hazard a guess when I am prompted to choose a pizza over a salad every Friday dinner time – but as humans, we make decisions based on emotion before trying to justify them with logic. Harvard professor Gerald Zaltman conducted research that found 95% of our decisions are subconscious, aka we're hard-wired to let our emotions drive our decision-making.[1]

So, that could mean impulse buying a sourdough Nduja pizza because you're having a bad day or choosing to buy your coffee from a small independent coffee shop because the founding story of a father and son rekindling their relationship over their love of a frappuccino made your eyes well up a bit. Or it could mean ordering a ring light you don't need because a TikTok influencer with 100 million followers told you to. Emotion first, logic second.

When you build a community – by creating resonance with other people on a human level – you speak to their experiences, their feelings and emotions. The result? You're *the* option, not *an* option, and therefore are in a pretty darn strong position to monetise your brand and charge more for your products and services (or get that payrise your boss has been putting off).

Communities also act as real-life social proof. If you have 5,000 people who like and engage with your content, and someone new finds your profile, then, guess what, they are much more likely to follow you. Why? Because people are fickle and we like to follow people that other people follow and like. Ninety-two per cent of people trust the opinion of another person over a company brand online[2] – it's why the likes of TripAdvisor and Amazon reviews exist. We think brands lie, so brands have had to create a mechanism to encourage people to co-sign products and services to legitimise them. Each like, comment, and message you get from your community is an endorsement that could convince someone else to click 'follow'. Told you – compound interest in a high-interest account.

The bottom line is that if you have 5,000 followers who all think you're great, the chances are that anyone new who finds you is going to think the same. When you focus on building tight-knit communities of superfans, you transition from having followers to friends, which creates a virtuous cycle that grows your profile. Chef's kiss.

Focus on actual engagement

Engagement is kind of a marketing buzzword. 'Oh, our audience is so engaged', 'How much engagement did you get?' 'My content isn't getting much engagement right now'. But what does that even mean?

Well, engagement is actually a pretty easy formula. Your engagement rate is calculated as:

The total number of interactions your content receives ÷ your total number of followers × 100% = your engagement rate.

In simple terms, it's a measure of how well your personal brand content performs independently of your follower count, aka focus on how engaged people are in what you have to say vs. how many people are listening to you say it. School curriculums could learn a thing or two about that.

Are people interacting with you? Are members of your community interacting with one another? An unreal measure of engagement in your content is when you see people having conversations in your comment sections, debating the topic of your content, or celebrating one another. When you get this level of engagement, it shows that people not only like your content, but that they also like *you*. Building a community isn't about you, but it is about you facilitating a place where people can connect with other people like *them*. The best way to do that is by using the method I've been using throughout this book:

1. Define your goal.

2. Work out who you need to attract to make that goal happen.

3. Share content that those people find interesting and valuable.

4. Create resonance through humanising your content's delivery.

5. Deliver that content on a platform your community are already on.

6. Engage with the people who have engaged with your content and learn what resonates with *them*.

7. Repeat 3–6 until you die.

Not really die. But you get my point – building a personal brand is not rocket science.

Communities come in many different forms – they can be online or in-person. A community could be a social media page, or it might be an open event. It could be a private members club, or a neighbourhood WhatsApp group. Soho House is an example of a paid-for community that comes with a level of status. Whether you're paying for the right to be able to buy expensive cocktails or roll your eyes at the latest group chat rant for free, the entire point of the community is that people need to feel like it's part of their identity. That they are proud to be a part of it. You want your community to wear their membership of your circle like a badge of honour. Our paid community, Get Klowt, includes an exclusive Slack channel. Anyone who is part of that community can ask or say anything they want to me, my team or the other members – and, more and more, we're seeing other members of the community answering those questions before I or my team have had a chance to jump in. That's a sign of a really good community – and Klowt is at the heart of it.

Engage to be engaging

A really simple way to start building any community is to show people you care about them. It's like making friends, really. Respond to messages, emails and comments on your content. Don't just post and run. Whenever someone gets in touch with you or mentions you – be responsive. Feed back into the ecosystem you're trying to take from.

I can imagine you're reading this and saying, 'Like, really? I have to respond to every comment?' – and yes, yes, you do at the beginning. Do you seriously mean to tell me that you've got to Chapter 9 in this book about taking control of your life, turning your story into a competitive advantage by building your personal brand and you don't have five minutes a day to respond to people's comments that you're so desperately asking them to give? Grow up. No, seriously, grow up. Or put this book down, because I am not here to tell you that this stuff is easy. Is it simple? Yes. Easy? Nope. But that is why it's such a huge opportunity.

No one else has the stomach, nor the conviction to, day in and day out, post content that will resonate with human beings and then make the time (we all can) to respond to people when they do engage with what they're posting. It's too much work. Just like going to the gym to get the body of your dreams, and attract the partner you've always wanted and live until the ripe old age of 90 having had an amazing life that you were completely in control of, are too much work. Everything is hard work. You get to choose your hard. So, what's it going to be?

When I first started to build my personal brand, I used to spend hours responding to people who contacted me – at one stage I had about 1,000 messages per week going into my LinkedIn inbox. I made a point of going back to all of them, even if it took me weeks to do so. To this day, I still respond to everyone who sends me a message. I'm lucky that I now have an amazing EA whom I trust and who responds on my behalf to messages, and an incredible Community Growth Executive who helps me post my content. This isn't insincere – she is very transparent in telling people that she's responding on my behalf – but I still take time out to respond to messages and speak to people in my inbox. And I take the time out of my day to meet with people virtually if they feel like they want my help.

If you want to hand this part of building your community over to someone else, you can, but why would you? If you want to know what your community wants to hear about or learn from, you have to be at the forefront of it. Not another person. When you're clear, and the community is growing – cool, delegate some tasks. But you can't outsource your personality completely, it's *your* personality. *Your* reputation. No one else's. And I say that while running a personal branding agency that writes and posts content on other people's behalf.

So spend that time – make that time, for God's sake – to respond to people's comments and learn what people want to know about you. When you first start building your personal brand, it's very unlikely that you'll receive thousands of comments or Direct Messages that you have to respond to. I do – humble brag – which is why I need help. But I didn't for a long time, so your argument of 'I don't have time' will not be accepted in this court of law. And if and when you do reach a point where your community has grown so big that you need some help? Create a list of FAQs and have a virtual assistant respond to people on your behalf. Personally, I believe it's disingenuous for my EA to respond as me, so she is always open about the fact that she's replying on my behalf. And that is why people trust my personal brand. Authenticity and transparency are key.

I know there are plenty of famous people and influencers who pretend they're the ones engaging with the people in their community when in reality it's their team, and, sure, it makes people feel special. And, wow, manpower makes a big difference to your growth trajectory, but it just doesn't sit well with me. To build a community of people who care about you, you have to make them feel as though you care, and that's very difficult to do if you're not responding to them sincerely and honestly.

In my opinion, a really good way to get your community bought into you and your content is to involve them in your decision-making. For example, before I published this book, I asked my audience which covers they preferred. My community loved it and we got 10 × the number of responses on that post than we had done that week. The Get Klowt platform came about because I posted a poll asking who would be prepared to pay for a community like the one I'd built, and, guess what, about 1,500 people voted yes. Their response was a big part of my decision to go ahead and build it. And why those people bought memberships.

A final way to encourage engagement in your content – and your brand – is to always use active language. Address people as 'you', identify as 'I' rather than saying 'we'. Using active language allows people to feel like you're addressing them directly, and therefore they will respond as such. Remember what I said about people 'buying' with emotion? Same thing here.

Give back

The idea of 'giving back to your community' can sound very self-indulgent. Like, you're not a charity. But as I said in Chapter 6, you don't have to be intelligent, or even educational, to be valuable to your community.

Do you remember that video that went viral – Pineapple Pen? If you haven't seen it, you've missed out. I sent that video to my brother recently in the family WhatsApp group because I knew he'd find it funny. We then proceeded to go back and forth sharing all this dumb, hilarious content that went viral on the internet years ago. That might sound ridiculous, but it's still a form of giving back – I gave him something that added value to his day. Maybe giving back to your community could be something as stupid as sharing a viral video from your childhood? Or it could be something as serious as donating $1 million to cancer research. Both of those are examples of 'giving back'.

Giving back can also mean replying to people's comments, or sending them content that you believe they will find valuable. It could be that you create a place where the members of your community can talk to one another and share skills they've learned – that's just another form of giving back. Your community can be an ecosystem where people can add perceived value, almost effortlessly – creating that kind of space is a form of giving back.

The point is, giving back doesn't have to be some grand philanthropic gesture. It can be as simple as giving people free, valuable information – or creating an environment where they can access valuable information – or sharing stupid viral Vine videos from the early 2,000s, for free.

And a way that you can do this is to share micro-versions of what you get paid to do. So, for example, I get paid to do a talk on personal branding. I will end-to-end teach you how to build your personal brand, in a workshop format. I will then chop that content up into micro videos and text posts online. If you were smart, you'd piece together all of my content and do it for yourself (like I have done in this book). And you'd be well within your rights to do so, and not pay a penny for it.

The thing is, most people don't do that. Statistically speaking, most of you will do jack all after reading this book. You'll think, 'Ah, that was interesting' and then it will go and collect dust on your bookshelf until your partner nags you enough to take it, and the others you've done the same with, to the local charity shop. And that is why you need to give 100% of your knowledge away for free, in micro format online, if you want to build a strong personal brand around a specific niche. Because of the 100 people that read your content, only one will actually action it. The rest will either wish they had, or will find the budget to pay you to do it for them.

It's very difficult for people to give you their credit card if they don't know what they're buying, but if you share your knowledge freely, you position yourself as someone worth buying from.

But as I've already said, sharing content doesn't mean you have to publish White Paper after White Paper. At Klowt we take an approach that we call 'atomising'. We take a longer piece of content like an article, or an interview, and break it down into tens, if not hundreds, of pieces of social media content. I'll talk more about my system for creating a lot of content quickly in Chapter 10.

Mirror your community

As I said right at the start of this chapter, you can't influence from above, you have to influence from within. What does that mean in practice? Well, one way is to mirror the language, behaviour, and so on of the people within your community. At this point in my personal branding journey, I'm producing content that is designed to appeal to and resonate with a mass audience – that means I explain even complex topics in simple language that's easy to understand. A doctor writing for a medical journal, meanwhile, will use a very different style and probably a lot of big words I don't understand to reflect the audience of a publication like that.

When I look at my personal brand, I can see how my language, tone and behaviour have evolved to mirror my changing community. When I look back at the content I produced when I first started working to build a following around my personal brand, it was aggressive, short, punchy and, in many ways, quite provocative because that's what my audience responded to – I was trying to attract CEOs, entrepreneurs and start-up founders who, generally, are headstrong, male and quite decisive.

Here's a post I did back then:

YEARS OF EXPERIENCE DO NOT = SKILL LEVEL.

And it certainly doesn't qualify someone for the job.

People have different learning curves.

What takes one person to learn in 5 years

Might take another 1 year.

Or even a couple of months.

And yet ALL the things that we hire on;

CVs,

YEARS OF EXPERIENCE,

PROOF YOU CAN FOLLOW INSTRUCTIONS,

none of these things qualify you for a job.

Or are even relevant to you being a decent hire.

So let's STOP demanding minimum years of experience.

Stop hiring on CVs.

And STOP making decisions based on things that DON'T qualify good work.

Because if you want to drive innovation and build authority –

Wouldn't you rather hire the person who'd figured it out in 1 year over 5?

Just a thought.

It's kind of aggressive, right? But at the time it worked. It got me in front of the CEOs of businesses like SkyBet, The National Lottery, *Fortune* magazine and *Management Today*. But it's not reflective of who I am any more, or of who my community is.

Here's a more recent post for comparison:

Klarna tried to sue me – or at least they threatened to.

The billion-dollar Buy Now Pay Later unicorn threatened to sue me because my tiny little start-up's brand was 'infringing on their trademark'.

I started my business in August 2020. The height of the pandemic. People were losing their jobs left, right, and centre, and I, being the crazy person I am, thought it was a great time to start a business.

But my idea worked.

People loved the idea of Klowt, and I landed our first two clients in week one. Fast forward to September 5th 2022.

'Just pinged you a crazy email,' my EA said on WhatsApp.

Reading the strongly worded, lawyer-written letter demanding we change our entire brand 'or else', my immediate response was laughter.

Surely this was a joke?

'Well, that's my LinkedIn post sorted for tomorrow,' I replied.

But it wasn't a joke; it was real – in big letter-headed print: 'Cease and Desist: Klarna'.

The issues they had were;

1. *Their brand name starts with a K. Our brand name starts with a K.*

   So naturally, they demanded we stop using our logo. . . (spoiler alert, you can't trademark a letter).

2. *Our brand colours were purple. Theirs were pink. They claimed they were, 'subjectively', the same colour.*

But none of this really matters, does it?

Because Klarna didn't really believe that Klowt infringed on their trademark or that purple and pink were the same colour. No, this entire exercise was about a billion-dollar company throwing its weight around. (And I know they're a billion-dollar company because they told me in their letter. . .).

It was bulls*it. I knew it. They knew it.

And yet, here I was – the founder of a start-up with a tiny team and tiny resources, staring down the barrel of a potentially lengthy and expensive defence case if I tried to fight it.

Could I even afford to fight it?

Klarna is a multi-billion dollar corporation with unlimited resources. Most founders probably would have thought it was best to concede and change their brand.

I am, however, pretty stubborn.

And I hate bullies.

So, I called my own legal 'team' (everyone needs a best friend who's a lawyer), who helped me draft a response, which told Klarna to go f*ck themselves – legally speaking.

I then recorded a video, which I posted to:

- LinkedIn

- TikTok

- YouTube

- Instagram

Reiterating how much I wanted them to go f*ck themselves. It even got picked up by the media.

And do you know what? We never heard back from them.

So now, I write this post in the corner of my home office, sitting next to – you guessed it – a framed copy of the Klarna Cease and Desist letter.

It's like a trophy.

A little memento to remind me – and now you – that people – and huge billion-dollar companies – will always try to bring you down when you start winning.

Never f*cking let them.

There is a fine balance to strike between shaping your content so that it drives engagement and becoming someone you're not to get likes. I walked on the knife-edge of this balance, back then. Often when I met people offline they would tell me that my actual personality was super friendly and my energy positive – something they'd not expected based on my content.

I did have a reason for my aggressive tone. I needed to stand out and attract a certain audience. If I'm honest though, there was also insecurity behind my approach. I thought that if I communicated aggressively, people might not like me – and that meant they didn't like me because of my *online persona*, not because of *who I was behind that*. It was like a self-defence barrier I put up to prevent myself from getting hurt. These days I write what I want, in the way that I say it. I know who I am, and the message that I want to share and to who and I don't let my ego get in the way of that pursuit. I am 100% OK with the consequences of what I say and how I say it, but there's a level of confidence I have now in who I am – a wonderful byproduct of building your personal brand online.

Look at Gary Vee as someone whose personal brand 'persona' has evolved as his community grew. If you watch some of his older content, it's so much more produced than it is today. It wasn't until he'd really built up his community that he started letting his authentic self come out – swearing, really challenging societal norms – and became the Gary we all know and love today.

If you look at the industry Gary was trying to infiltrate – executives, CEOs, Fortune 500 C-suite – you might think that being opinionated, direct and swearing would alienate them. But the reason he built trust with this community was because he was doing the opposite of everyone else. I told you about Steve Jobs' outfit choices being the opposite to his peers, resulting in a stronger brand. Gary is the same. Most C-level execs don't dare let anyone see them emotional, or, dare I say it, allow any chinks in the armour be visible. But by being himself, and communicating online in the same way he does to his team and in the boardroom, Gary has done what most C-level executives cannot – build trust.

It's important to view growing a personal brand and a community in unison – as you grow, you become more confident in yourself, you share what you want to share and your community is at a level at which they're ready to receive what you want to say. Authentically. You don't need to dive right in and bare your soul from the start – you can gradually peel back those layers, bringing the people in your community with you on that journey towards ever-greater authenticity. I told you, the most wonderful byproduct of this personal branding thing is you get so comfortable with who you are. And that alone is the greatest ROI.

Now, I'm not going to lie. Being yourself is scary. Especially online. There is a permanence to the things you say online in a way there is not at a dinner party or gathering of friends in the pub. But, get over it. You spend your entire life meeting the expectations of what other people think is right and appropriate for you – and that is why you're reading this book. You want to break free from the tyranny of having to fake who you are to please other people. And part of that process is to be unfiltered, unedited and truly authentic, even if people don't like it.

In fact, people not liking it is a wonderful thing. A community is not just defined by the people who like you. There is a great power in being disliked, as you can't be adored by the people who matter unless you're willing to be hated by the people who don't. So lean into your authentic self, let it act like a community filter and allow your tribe to find you. Your personality is like a sieve, it lets the people through that you want to let through, and filters out the ones you don't.

Deciding not to always put the most polished version of myself out there was pretty f**king scary. It was a ballsy move to decide to post a vlog of myself wearing pyjamas, with no make-up on and spots on my face (and a bad one, if you consult my mother). However, what I got off the back of putting myself out there in a raw, unfiltered way was an increased quality of people finding and liking my content, an increase in quality of potential team mates finding my business, an increase in quality of clients finding Klowt – and most importantly of all, an increase in confidence and self-love for me.

I don't have a mask on any more, and I know that some people don't like me – that's OK. But the people who do like me advocate even harder for me now than ever before – and it's because they can see I'm authentic. One of the messages I receive most frequently from people is, 'Thank you for saying the things we all want to say.'

I promise you, people will be grateful when you have the courage and confidence to share who you really are with them. They will reward you for having that courage, whether that's through likes and shares of your content, engagement, paying for your services or even public adoration.

People like to support people who are courageous, and it's very courageous to be yourself – especially on an online platform.

Click moments

As you take control of your personal brand, you'll attract the people you want to attract, and repel the ones you want to repel. The more authentic and open you are, the more the people in your community will come to like and trust you.

And this is how you create a community of friends, not followers, who will help get you into rooms you don't have access to. The most amazing thing about building a community is that it will grow organically if you nurture it right. So create content, share it – but add back into the ecosystem by responding to comments and messages. If you want people to give a s**t about you, you first have to give a s**t about them.

10

Building systems

I create upwards of 150 pieces of content per month. And this is how I have been able to generate 110 million views (at the time of publishing) on my content. I spend about one to two hours per week on my personal brand, and my distribution of it is vast. Because I have a system.

I actually don't think anything in life worth doing is worth doing without a system. The gym, you follow a workout schedule. Your work, you have a morning routine. Your partner, you have little habits to make sure they know you love them (I hope). Unless you have somehow managed to clone yourself or invent time travel, everything needs a system because even Beyoncé has only 24 hours in a day. Why would you treat your personal brand any differently? And, here's a secret that most social media 'experts' won't tell you: building a strong personal branding is 10% content, 90% consistency and volume of posting it.

Trust me when I say this is a *numbers* game. The only reason you're reading my book right now is because I have posted *so* much and *so* consistently over the course of four years, that Wiley thought it would be a great idea to pay me to write a book about it. Oh, the power of compound brand interest.

I'm not saying anything particularly unique – personal branding is the second-highest followed hashtag on LinkedIn and I am *far* from the only person who talks about it. But I have been talking about it *more* and for a lot longer than many other people, which is how I've been able to cut through the noise.

Aside from the time you save (you're welcome), a nice little benefit of having a system to create your personal brand content is that it stops you overthinking. It removes the doubt, the procrastination, the 'should this have the word "amazing" or "fabulous"' nonsense that we all do when we're trying to convey something important. Having a plan means you avoid creating content at the last minute when your cortisol levels could power a SpaceX flight – and your mind is questioning even the most basics of thoughts. Or worse, talks you out of posting your thoughts at all.

So, without further ado. My system.

Create a cornerstone

A cornerstone piece of content is ideally a long-form piece of content that you produce weekly, or even monthly, that all your other content can come back to. It could be an article, or a video series, a book, or a podcast. My cornerstone content is *Branded by Amelia Sordell*. Every single piece of content, outside of my weekly YouTube vlog, pretty much, comes from this.

The premise of the podcast is to interview people who've built strong personal brands or strong company brands, and uncover what it takes to do the same. Learn from their mistakes, their triumphs, their wins and their losses. To connect with them on a human level and tell their story to an audience of, to be honest, f**king amazing listeners and viewers (shout out Branded crew). But in reality? It's a bloody good excuse to talk to people about the two topics that I talk most about – personal branding and entrepreneurship.

Interviewing these incredible people from influencers, to FTSE CEOs and start-up founders, I get the opportunity to bounce off incredible people, incredible ideas – and add my two cents too. I network, build relationships and am able to build relationships with their audience too. But the podcast itself doesn't actually get crazy downloads. I think people think that by starting an interesting podcast, you'll automatically get interesting guests and therefore views. Wrong. A podcast isn't meant to be a destination, it's meant to be a channel of distribution – or if you're like me, the basis of all your other content, so you never have to create anything ever again.

Could you write a newsletter every week? Produce a vlog series, or have a podcast like me? I like podcasting because I get an excuse to meet people and bounce off them. So what is your cornerstone?

Atomise your content

Atomise. Verb. To reduce something to atoms.

Or in my case, blow up one long-form piece of content into tens, if not hundreds, of pieces of micro content for social media. This is why I have a podcast. Who the hell has hours a week to spend creating new content? Not me. And I certainly don't want to. I want to rock up, meet and interview amazing people, share cool ideas and get back to work. And that is what I do. And through that process of interviewing people for the podcast once a week, I am able to squeeze out hundreds of unique pieces of micro content that then get shared on LinkedIn, TikTok, Instagram, Pinterest and YouTube.

These could be micro videos, transcribed LinkedIn posts, Pinterest graphics of quotes – smaller versions of particular topics for YouTube. It's like the master stock that a good restaurant has in a kitchen. On its own, it's tasty, but it's the basis for every other dish in the place. The only real work you need to do is contextualise that micro content for the platform you're sharing it on. Simple and efficient. I love this process for us all.

So here's my system.

1. Record 1 × podcast.

2. Post the podcast video on YouTube channel.

3. Use an AI tool to chop up the podcast into 20 micro clips for TikTok.

4. Transcribe those 20 micro clips and turn them into LinkedIn posts.

5. Pull out 30 soundbites from the total micro clips, and turn them into 30 Tweets.

6. Screenshot those 30 Tweets and reshare them on Instagram.

7. Condense those original 20 transcribed micro clips into X (Twitter) threads.

8. Repurpose the short videos you've posted on TikTok as Instagram Reels.

9. Repurpose your 20 LinkedIn posts as Instagram captions and share with relevant pictures.

10. Pitch yourself onto another podcast and repeat.

1 Podcast + 1 YouTube + 20 TikToks + 20 LinkedIn Posts + 30 Tweets + 30 Instagram Threads posts + 20 × Threads + 20 Instagram Reels + 20 Instagram captions = 162 pieces of content.

But you don't need a podcast to replicate this method. Here is how you can do this right now.

1. Write down 10 questions you get asked frequently. Think about your answers, perhaps make some notes, and then grab your phone and video yourself answering each question. Even if you spend as much as ten minutes answering each one, that's less than two hours of your time.

2. You can turn each of the answers you've recorded into a five- to ten-minute YouTube video. That's 10 pieces of content straight out the gate.

3. Then you can watch each of your 10 videos and pull out the two most interesting points from each one. Make a note of the time stamp in the video and edit those points into micro videos, for TikTok and Instagram. That's a further 20 pieces of content. (And before you make excuses, CapCut is an idiot-proof video editor for your phone. And if even that's beyond you, hire a cheap freelancer on Fiverr.)

4. Transcribe your initial 10 YouTube videos and edit those to become posts for LinkedIn.

5. You can do the same with each micro video to give you soundbites for either LinkedIn or X (formerly Twitter).

6. If you are posting on X (formerly Twitter), you can screenshot these posts, and then reshare them on LinkedIn or Instagram.

Ah, voilà! A replicable system that allows you to spend as little time as possible creating as much content as possible, which is aligned to your audience and goal. You're welcome. Now, as payment, please leave this book a review on Amazon.

When you count all that content up, from just one two-hour recording session, you could end up with a whopping 30 videos, 10 LinkedIn posts and 20 soundbites/quotes to post. If you screenshot posts on one platform and reshare them on another social media site, you are stretching that content even further.

And once you've shared this content, you can then use the feedback from it to inform your next batch of questions. Another batch of ideas with minimal effort – your audience literally telling you what they want you to say. You can continue doing this indefinitely – and the more comfortable you get with recording yourself on video, and doing the editing, the more content you'll be able to produce.

If you want to supercharge this process, end each post or video with a question – 'Was this helpful?', 'What would you do?', 'Opinion?'. This encourages engagement, as I've said earlier in the book – check. But it also tells your audience to give you their thoughts and questions = more content ideas for you. Check, check.

One of the things I've been doing recently is content theming my months. So, if you're a life coach, for example, you could do a month exclusively on confidence building – and every post you create centres on that topic from a different angle, lens or perspective. The following month you might do goal setting, which would mean sharing practical tips on what strong goals look like, how to set them and how to hold yourself accountable for going after them. It keeps you, your content and your message consistent and means that your audience gets really deep into what you have to say because it's all you're saying for a month. Gary Vee does this really well.

Best part about this entire exercise of creating micro from long-form content? You can re-do this in a few months' time and pull out the best bits from your older content and reshare them on the same social platforms in a slightly different format. I do this often. Remix, repurpose, reshare. Not repurposing your content is like only wearing a great outfit once.

Create once, distribute a thousand times. I love a system, don't you?

Consume content to create it

The biggest barrier people have to building their personal brand outside of having the balls to start building it, is knowing what to say. Even people with big personal brands struggle with content ideas. Writer's block IS a thing.

And I'm sure if you've tried to build your brand before that you'll know what I mean. You schedule time in your diary, you get to said time and there is nothing but air in your head. I've been there. But I think the expectation we put on ourselves to be creative out of thin air is wild. When was the last time you read a fiction book? Or had a daydream? Or had an interesting conversation? Today? If you're not doing these things, how on earth do you expect to be inspired to create? You have to consume content if you want to create it, which means instead of doom-scrolling cat pages on TikTok at 3 a.m. you need to get a bit more strategic in how you spend your time online.

I dedicate a few hours a week to what I call 'intentional scrolling'. I even encourage it with my team. We have weekly trend sessions where people bring ideas of content they've seen and we talk about which client it would be awesome for. When you're trying to create content, it's so hard to do this without first being inspired. Without consuming things that inspire you, you can't yourself be inspiring. It's the paradox of creativity. Want to be creative? Go do creative things.

It's the same principle that I apply to the food I eat – I know that if I eat junk food all the time, I'll look and feel rubbish. I also know that if I give my body healthy food, I'll look and feel amazing. My mind – and your mind – are the same. If you go into a session to create your cornerstone content with a mind full of ideas that have been inspired by the content you've been consuming, you will come out of that session with excellent content. You get out what you feed in, capiche?

This doesn't have to mean you *just* spend hours online scrolling through social media. You can get great inspiration from the interactions you have every day. Document everything. I screenshot articles, messages, I leave myself voice notes of cool conversations I've had or write notes down after a shower thought or podcast. Content and inspiration for it are everywhere, you just need to know where to look.

And the best part of documenting everything is you never run out of things to say. It's all there, right in the notes section of your phone. I have 1847 notes of content ideas. Don't judge me – I have a lot of things to say.

Remember, none of us can be inspired *just* because someone is telling us to be inspired – we're not performing monkeys. We are human beings. But the more you consume interesting content, the more you can create it.

A system for content distribution

Creating content is only half of the battle. Once you have content, you need a system to distribute it. You know, which post is going where and when? This will help you stay consistent – and if you follow the same formula repeatedly, it acts like a funnel. Magic.

Because I am in the business of giving 100% of my knowledge away for free (unless you paid for this book, in which case, thank you for your custom), below is the method I use to drive brand awareness to my personal brand and leads into my DMs. It's the model that I used to build my business from $0 to $1.3 million in annual inbound revenue in three years. It's actually quite simple.

Monday: post a personal post

This is where you tell your story. Share about how you founded your business, or talk about your career journey, how you love to cycle and what 'balance' means to you. Doesn't matter really, provided it shows people who you are as a person. I talk a lot about failure, because it's my 'thing' (I spent most of my high school years in detention, after all), but for you, it could be your obsession with tea over coffee (we've spoken about this before, and I'm starting to get concerned for your sanity).

Tuesday: post related to your expertise

This is where you give your knowledge away for free or comment on a trending topic related to your niche. Add your expertise, and your why. Ask people to give their opinions on it in the comments.

Wednesday: post related to your expertise, but more in depth

For me, this is where you do breakdowns, in-depth analysis, how-to guides and such. This is the layer deeper than your previous day's post.

Thursday: post a results post

This is proof that what I'm talking about is legit. It might be a screenshot of data from a client who had great results, or a story about how you took something from A–Z and how you did it. This is the 'hook' that gets people into your DMs if they're the right fit.

Friday: post a personal post, again

Why does this work? Well, by starting my cycle with something personal, I'm appealing to a mass audience – I am pulling the dopamine lever to get as many people looking at my content and profile as possible. Then, as soon as I post about personal branding on Tuesday, I lose the people who aren't interested in hearing about that topic. Not a bad thing, by the way. By posting the same type of content again the following day, I reduce the numbers further. Now I've squeezed a vast number of people into a much smaller group – but these are all people who are absolutely interested in what I have to say and much more engaged as a result.

On Thursday I show them how good I am with real-life results, and then on Friday I hit them with another personal post. Reminding people of why it's *me* they like, not someone else who does the same thing. This is *so* important because the people left in my funnel at this point may want to buy from me. And that is what this is, by the way. A funnel.

Rinse and repeat this cycle – if the people seeing your content are your ideal customers, they'll pop out at the end eventually.

Following this formula also makes it really, really easy for you to identify what content you need to create on a weekly or monthly basis to enable you to execute consistently, at a very high level. And once you have a system, it's so much easier to actually get your act together and share the content you need to share to get the results you want to get.

The key to sticking to this cadence is marking out time in your diary for content creation – and, as you've seen, it doesn't have to be hours and hours each week or month. Depending on what your cornerstone content of choice is, you could do 30 minutes a week or two hours a month. Just figure out what works for you, and stick to the formula.

By the way, when you post at this rate consistently, people will also start to expect to see content from you, and that means they will notice if you don't post. Over Christmas 2023, I took a break from posting because I was tired and burnt out for the hundredth time since starting the business. The glamorous life of an entrepreneur. But when I went back on my social media I had messages from people asking if they'd missed posts from me – they noticed I had gone. Pretty good sign people care, don't you think?

And, yes, you need to post consistently. Do you need to post when you're going on vacation like some kind of influencer in the wild? No. You can take a break without damaging your personal brand growth. So, go get a Pina Colada on a beach somewhere, you deserve it.

Comments are content, too

Content isn't just the things that you post on your social media, it's also the thoughts that you add to other people's posts and the way in which you engage with other people's content. This is usually comments, but it could also be by reposting or sharing something that you think is cool.

Commenting on other people's stuff is actually the easiest way to build a personal brand and expand your network with people who otherwise wouldn't ever have come across you or your content.

My 9 × 3 rule:

1. Find **9** thought leaders and influencers with audiences of people that you want to reach.

2. Spend **9** minutes per day. . .

3. Interacting or commenting on **9** different posts.

This will gain you visibility. This will grow your audience. And if you're pairing this strategy with posting content, this will help you build an incredibly strong personal brand (and win a lot of inbound opportunities).

Nine minutes a day is nothing. That's probably how long you're messing around on Instagram for while you wait for your coffee to brew. The beauty of this is that because you're engaging with nine different people's content, you're contributing to the conversation and content ecosystem in your niche. The comments you leave will more than likely get some engagement, and that will introduce you to new audiences. The key is to make sure you're commenting on relevant content and that you're ideally finding people whose audience is similar to the one you are trying to appeal to.

At Klowt we have one client who gets more engagement on the comments he leaves on other people's content than he does on his own content. This is great. Why? Well, it shows that people are interested in what he has to say and the more he does this, the more new people will discover him. They will see his name pop up in multiple conversations and out of curiosity will then look at his content. The result? He'll get more eyeballs on his content and, *provided it's good*, will end up with more people following him.

So ask questions, add to the conversation – ask the original poster why they came to that conclusion. Disagree with them! I won a client once by disagreeing with their post in the comments section. Dare to be authentic. My top tip is to not only share an opinion but to *end your comment with a question.*

Like, 'It's really interesting that you came to that conclusion. My thought process behind it is [share your thought process]. How did you get to yours?' Now the original poster has a reason to engage with you. Algorithmically, this is great. It means your comment will be seen by more people – more people that you want to attract. And the best part is, you can continue that conversation and invite other people to be a part of it too. If you can manage to do that nine times a day, you're laughing.

Commenting on nine different posts from nine different people is the ideal situation. The crème de la crème. But even if you only leave one comment on one other person's post each day, and you do that a few times in a week, you will still see a difference in the number of people finding you and engaging with your own content.

But can I be honest? Don't use that as a cop out. If you've got enough time to get to this point in the book – and this deep into your new approach to life – then you have nine minutes a day to post comments on other people's stuff.

LinkedIn pro tip

If you want to encourage people to follow you vs. connect with you (which you should, because LinkedIn restricts you to a maximum of 30,000 connections and trust me, it's a pain in the ass to disconnect from undesirable connections), change your 'connect' button to a 'follow' button. That doesn't mean people can't connect with you, *they can*, it's just a more lengthy process. This means you grow your audience faster, because you don't have to accept them as a connection, and you get to maintain whose content appears in *your* feed. Winning.

As much as I talk about 'don't worry about followers', they are important, because they're the kind of tangible indication that you – and your content – are worth the hype to people who've never seen you or it, yet. But connections are like the inner sanctum on LinkedIn, so use them sparingly. And if anyone else tries to connect with you, you can politely request that they follow you instead. Here's how I respond to unrequited connection requests now I have quite literally reached my limit.

Thank you so much for connecting, but I've maxed out of connections right now. I'd love to stay in touch so follow me and we can stay connected.

Most people understand how LinkedIn works in this respect, and if you are polite and send them a message, they don't feel snubbed and will happily follow you.

Repurpose, recycle, remix

Earlier in this chapter I talked about atomising your content – an A-grade formula, if you ask me. This is basically a fancy way of saying 'repurpose'. Repurposing is much broader than just breaking a long piece of content into shorter chunks though. It can work the other way too – perhaps you made a really insightful point on a podcast, which you can then use as a foundation for a piece of cornerstone content? Repurposing is, as the name suggests, taking a piece of content and turning it into another piece of content in a different format.

Recycling is slightly different. This is when you post the same piece of content more than once. The key is to make sure you leave a decent amount of time – usually a few months is enough – between each post. If your content isn't time-sensitive, resonates with your audience and is already well put together, repost it. Don't be a clever idiot who only posts 'original' content – there are no medals for those kinds of people. Only time saps from constantly creating because your ego is too big to find short cuts.

Personally, I've posted '*Not repurposing your content is like buying a great outfit and only wearing it once*' about seven times now. It always does well.

As I explained in Chapter 6, only a tiny percentage of your followers will see the content you post on social media, so resharing posts that have done well is a great way to make sure more people see them. I have a handful of posts I have reshared repeatedly and no one has ever contacted me and said, 'You've posted that before.'

Remixing is when you take a piece of content that did well and rework it a bit so that you're sharing the same message slightly differently. You might do that to improve a post's performance, or to ensure it performs well across lots and lots of channels. Or add in some time-sensitive detail that makes it relevant again.

Basically, the entire point of repurposing, recycling and remixing is getting the maximum amount of mileage out of a single piece of content. I meant it literally when I said create once, distribute a thousand times.

I've been talking about the same things for five years now. And that is why I am known for talking about those things. If you want to be famous, you have to be famous for something – and to be famous for something, you have to talk about that thing all the time.

The metrics that matter

I had written a lengthy section about performance, and metrics and what you need to measure and why, but, to be honest, there are only really three things that matter when building your personal brand online:

- **Impressions** – Aka views on your content, but what counts as an impression will vary between social media platforms. For example, on LinkedIn an impression on a video is counted as anyone who watched it for seven seconds or longer. But on Instagram, whenever your content appears in another person's feed, that counts as an impression.

- **Engagement rate** – We did this maths lesson before. The total number of interactions your content receives ÷ your total number of followers × 100% = your engagement rate. On LinkedIn, a good engagement rate is about 1.5% (average is 0.5). That might sound quite low, but remember that on average only 3% of your followers see your content. At Klowt, we aim for an engagement rate of between 0.5% and 3% for our clients.

- **Audience profile** – Essentially *who* is following you. This comes back to creating fans not followers. I would rather have 50 followers who are diehard fans who were exactly who I wanted to have in my network than 50,000 followers who have no interest in buying what I'm selling.

Why do these matter? Well, impressions mean your content is landing with someone. Anyone. Even if it's your mum to start with. What I can't tell you is what a 'good' number of impressions looks like because that *very much* depends on how many followers you have. If you've only got 50 followers and are getting 50 impressions on every piece of content, you're smashing it. If you have 500,000 followers and you're only getting 50 impressions per piece of content, then I cannot help you.

Before you start using this as a barometer of your content's performance, my advice is to define what good looks like for *you*. Post for one month, see what the baseline impressions are and go from there.

Impressions are stunning – they make you look cool to your friends when you go viral. But impressions aren't the most important thing. You need to look at the quality of your audience as a priority really, because if you're a B2B marketer going viral every week, looking to attract other marketers, but all your audience are die-hard Harry Potter fans, you might need to rethink your strategy.

In my opinion, your audience profile is the most important metric when it comes to measuring the performance of your personal brand. It is second only to the inbound opportunities you get sliding into your DMs. However, if I'm honest, if you have the right audience profile, inbound opportunities will follow.

Every month I look at what did well and what didn't across all my social media accounts and then optimise my content off the back of it. I recently discovered that my best performing content on Instagram was of me goofing around to trending audios, and content of me speaking on stage. So we optimised for that and went from 8,000 followers to 42,000 followers in a few months.

Measurement tools

LinkedIn: ShieldApp AI. One of the only platforms that allows you to see metrics from your personal profile vs. a company's. It also allows you to tag up your content so you can find patterns across mediums, topics and times you've posted so you can really optimise on a granular level. Big fan. They should, in fact, sponsor me.

I could give you a bunch of measurement tools for the other channels, brands typically use Hootsuite or Sprout Social, but, to be honest, they're usually expensive and if you're only worried about your personal brand, it doesn't take a genius to look at the in-app analytics and work out what's doing well and what isn't.

Signs your system is working

How will you know when your content system is working? When opportunities start landing in your inbox without you feeling as though you've had to work for them. I've never had a problem with generating leads or opportunities. They just come to me. That isn't because I am lucky (I am), it's because I've built a system that does all the heavy lifting. I don't have to concentrate on convincing people to work with us, because they're already convinced. The dream, right? Well, it's not a dream. It's an outcome from a well-executed plan delivered consistently.

Of course, though, you and I both know that building healthy new habits takes hard work. Blah blah. Staying hydrated and sane is a task enough for me most days. So don't let the key takeaway from this book be 'Wow, this is amazing, I need to do this', only to post content for three weeks and give up. Don't be a statistic. If you want inbound opportunities; if you want freedom to work with who you want to work with; if you want to take control of your life and stop waiting for other people to give you permission to live the life that you want to live, you need to take action. And you need to take action, consistently. It's not sexy, it's not cool – but it works. And if you implement everything you've learned in this book, in 12 months' time you'll have used your story to win a competitive advantage. You'll be in control of your reputation, your personal brand – and your life. And that, my friends, is why I wrote this book.

I no longer see social media as a source of entertainment or fun – it's a tool I've used to reach millions of people. I'm leveraging where people spend most of their time, to get them to spend their time on me. When you make content creation a habit, you view your use of social media differently – personally I see social media as part of my job. It's no longer a place where I go to seek validation for my personality, it's somewhere I go to distribute it. And that's an incredibly healthy place to be. It's also why you'll *rarely* find me mindlessly scrolling these days. I'm mentally healthier and have a lot more time (who knew TikTok was such a time sap?) than I had before. I've boosted my confidence – I genuinely love the skin I'm in. The 18-year-old me with an eating disorder and obscene insecurities would be shocked.

When you take control of your personal brand and systemise it, you can change your whole relationship with social media – and with yourself.

For many people, social media feels like a necessary evil. It certainly did for me before I went on this journey. In reality, if you use it in the right ways, it can be a really great tool to grow your personal brand, your business *and* your confidence. It's changed my life, really. I want it to change yours too.

Click moments

Who has time to create a post every day and share it on time? Not me. I've had over 110 million views online (at the time of writing) and I know that is going to compound. But I spend so little time on social media – or creating content. Document your ideas, define your cornerstone long-form content and your distribution channels and get to work. Atomise your content and follow the 9 × 3 rule on days you post. Monitor, measure and optimise your content and repeat. It's simple really. And that is why people think it's so hard.

11

Building brand equity

Earlier in the book I said building your personal brand is a lot like paying money into a high-interest account. Imagine that account had 15% interest – even if you're only paying in $1 per day, at the end of 12 months you'd have $54.75 more than you started with. Do that for 10 years, you'd have $8522.49. All from paying in just $1 a day.

And that is how your personal brand works. I started off by getting one like here, two likes there – now I get an average of a couple of hundred to a couple of thousand per post, depending on the platform. That has compounded into over 110 million views, and $4 million in inbound revenue. That's insane – all from just posting once a day online.

The more views, engagement, speaking gigs, podcast appearances and one-to-one interactions you can have with people, the more your brand equity will grow – provided those interactions are *meaningful, memorable and positive.*

I tell clients, *your personal brand is an asset.* And I'm not exaggerating. The more you can invest in yours, the more valuable it is going to become – you're building brand equity with every piece of content you post, every appearance you make and every message you send. But just as not every 'bank' account offers the same interest rates, not every activity for personal branding is equal. You need to work out what the right activities are for you, to make sure you're getting the most out of them.

And the most valuable activities you can do for your personal brand depend entirely on what you're trying to achieve, the industry you're in and the community you're trying to build your personal brand in. I said in Chapter 10, once you get going with the cadence of building your brand, you need to spend time reviewing what is working and what is not to ensure you're always on the hunt for a better return on investment (ROI) on where you're spending your time and the content that you're creating.

If you're a business owner, the way in which you monetise your personal brand might be obvious – selling your product or service. That was very much the strategy I used when I started and grew Klowt. For three years, I built my personal brand around being known for entrepreneurship, business and personal branding to get the attention of founders and execs who would help me sell my services to them. Talking about business got them into my orbit, sharing content on personal branding turned them into customers. And I did that pretty simply – by sharing personal branding advice, tips and steps that other people could take to achieve the same results I had. I spoke from experience and shared my knowledge with the story of how I acquired it. This positioned me as a credible authority in the personal branding space and – because I gave *so* much information away for free – I was the only option on people's minds when they were ready to buy.

But *you* might not have a product or service to sell. You might not even run a business, and why should you? It's exhausting. Just ask your boss. When I first started building my personal brand, I didn't do it to generate leads for my business – I was employed. And that personal brand I built enabled me to get headhunted, join an incredible business – 11 Investments, which I spoke about right at the beginning of this book – and kickstarted my journey to business ownership, and ultimately freedom. *Your* sole purpose with personal branding might be to appear as a guest on more podcasts, to get more speaking engagements, or even to get a new job. Your version of monetisation might not actually be about making any money yet, but instead capitalising on your credibility and platform to get you into rooms you can't currently get into.

Go back to the goals you set in Chapter 2. Re-read your mission statement. This is the outcome you're looking for – and this is what you can use to assess how much equity you've built up in your personal brand. So, if you don't want to make money out of your personal brand, what do you want? Is it increased recognition? People to know who you are? Speaking engagements?

If it is speaking gigs, your personal brand needs to be geared around presenting you as a really f**king great speaker. So your 'personal branding activities' need to be centred around that. Pitch yourself as a guest on people's podcasts, add the word 'speaker' to your bio. Record any events that you do and post the micro content on your social media. The more you can present yourself as a speaker, the more people will see you as one. And the more you will be invited to speak at events – and eventually get paid to do it.

My other piece of advice is, do not wait to be asked to be a speaker – be proactive. Go out there and pitch yourself to speak on the stages you want to appear on. Send out emails to the hosts of podcasts you want to be on. Be confident. *Own* your expertise. Don't wait for permission to become a thought leader – give yourself the permission.

From my personal branding playbook: crafting a pitch bio

Your pitch bio needs to include the sexy parts of your story that will get people interested in who you are, what you do – and why you, specifically, are a worthwhile speaker. Mine includes why I founded my business, some of my big moments of failure, my journey over the last four years and, finally, the message I want to share with the world.

I've spoken about podcasts a lot in this book – maybe I should do another one just on how to leverage a podcast to become a thought leader, however, we're here to talk about personal branding. And podcasts are a bloody good way to build your brand. It's pretty simple really, make a list of 50 podcasts that have audiences of people you're trying to reach – we rank these at Klowt by tier. So tier one being the big ones, I'm talking millions of downloads, famous hosts – and guests. The ultimate prize. These go all the way down to tier three. Tier three podcasts are the ones with little fame outside of a small, niche audience and who are always looking for interesting people to talk to – and to build your personal brand, you first have to start there.

There is a *value exchange* that happens in this arrangement. You're collaborating with other creators for mutual benefits. They have you on their platform, you get to talk about you. Win, win. It is also why I *don't ever* charge for appearing on other people's podcasts. It's wild to think that people do. I'll never forget, I asked a pretty well-known CEO to appear on my podcast *Branded By Amelia Sordell* – they replied and said absolutely, but that it would cost me £350. The thing is, I'd have happily paid for their time, but the way they responded to the proposal with an invoice felt, well, icky. And totally misaligned to my values of give, give, give, give, give then ask. So I declined and we found another guest. That CEO has since approached us to be a guest again. *Your* payment for appearing on a podcast is the content creation you get in return – you are going to get a beautifully created long-form piece of content that you can share on your channels and atomise into pieces of micro content for your social media. You get a lovely produced showreel to share, so that people can see you as a great guest – and a great speaker. And if the podcast host is decent, they will also be sharing your content and tagging you in their posts. A great way to piggyback off other people's networks.

Your payment is the attention. To my mind, that's far more valuable than money.

Personal brands create stronger business brands

So many businesses have stuffy social media policies, with the intention of gagging their employees or putting them off posting online. That is a really dumb decision. Individuals within a business receive 561% more reach online than a company brand and 8 × more engagement.[1] And if your goal with building a brand strategy of any kind is to attract talent or customers, it seems kind of stupid to ignore the quickest route to that market – your people. Let's look at this from the perspective of attracting candidates for job roles in your business, which means the success of any personal branding activity would be measured in the number and quality of inbound job applications.

And it's pretty easy to track whether or not personal branding has had an impact on that as a goal. It doesn't take a genius to look at where job applications have come from, or where careers page visits originate. You can draw pretty solid conclusions against people posting content = increased employer brand awareness and conversations. To get your team to really activate your employer brand, you need to encourage them to talk about their work, their lives, and ultimately their role in your business. Through sharing their experiences, they ultimately win attention from like-minded people (and potentially other candidates) and with a platform like LinkedIn specifically, it ranks members' content above sponsors' ads and company page updates. So if your team are not posting, no one will visit your company page to see that you're hiring anyway.

Why is this so important? Well, brands lie. And people know they lie – which is why Glassdoor exists. But Glassdoor also lies, because almost all Glassdoor reviews are either incentivised by the company to inauthentically boost the ratings, or are only left by disgruntled employees. Which means candidates are increasingly looking to LinkedIn for honest, authentic takes from present employees on what it's like to actually work at a business.

You've got to build a culture of personal branding within your organisation – which, if you remember, is what my employer failed to embrace when I started this journey. The more you empower your team to build their personal brands, the more attention a business gets, the more applicants they have applying – and the more leads they generate. Attention via your employees helps you stand out, for all the right reasons.

And, look, people do leave. I left my employer – his number one objection was having people post content on LinkedIn. But if an employee builds a really strong personal brand through your business and then leaves, their brand will still be associated with your business. And you still benefit from all the attention they got during the time they were with you. For a year after I left the recruitment agency I worked for, I was still being approached by people who said, 'Oh, you're the woman from that business.' People still associated me with that company because that was where I'd built up my personal brand. And thus, the company benefited from my personal brand long after I left.

Basically, employees with strong personal brands are an opportunity, not a threat.

Know your worth

I get asked a lot about how to know what to charge for speaking gigs, talks and appearances. My honest answer? Whatever gets me excited to do the damn thing. $500? $1,000? $15,000? Then work out your pricing structure based on that. How I started was by charging $500, and then incrementally increasing the fee each year until I got to a point where it was an outrageous enough number that I was excited, but it still made economical sense to any profitable business. There's a balance. And, of course, there are things I do for free. I said earlier, not every transaction needs money to change hands. Some of the biggest stages I've spoken on were pro bono, but they were fun. The audience was right – and they led to business (and content creation) off the back of it. That's way more valuable than $500 or even $5,000.

In short, know your worth – but also know what it is worth being creative with your negotiations for. But if you are going to charge, make sure it's fairly for your time, effort and travel costs. Is it a custom talk, or one you do a lot? My prices differ for both. At the time of writing, I have three off-the-shelf talks that I can deliver with very little preparation because I know them by heart and all the slides and visual aids have already been created. So, I charge less.

However, if someone wants me to come into their business and deliver a workshop or bespoke talk, then I charge more. More effort, more work, more money. Don't get me wrong, I didn't start out charging reassuringly expensive rates – I learned over the years what I felt was exciting, and what my customers felt was fair based on value.

Whatever you decide to charge for speaking gigs or talks, say it with your chest. If you can't tell someone your rates confidently to their face, follow up with an email, where you can better control the tone of delivery. No one trusts someone who pussyfoots around their fees.

Influencer or thought leader?

Influencer or thought leader? Because there is a difference. One has amassed a following of people, and is paid to promote products and services to those people. A bit like a beautiful, human billboard. A thought leader is someone who promotes ideas, not products. There is no right or wrong to either – they're just different. Let me be clear, everyone has influence. You have influence, your dog has influence, my kids definitely have influence when they're negotiating bedtime with me on a Friday night, but there is a distinct difference between those who are paid to be influential, and those who are influential – and get paid.

I've only ever done one paid partnership at the time of writing this book. One. I've been asked by dozens of brands to share their products and services on my pages – and said no to a lot of money as a result, but I'm not trying to be an influencer. I want to spread a message, and my 'payment' in return for that is hopefully clients to my agency, consulting business, and Get Klowt platform. And, most importantly, inspiring you to build *your* brand.

So if *you* are positioning yourself as a thought leader, it's important to think carefully about how you respond to requests for endorsements. There is nothing wrong with being paid for sharing a product or service with your community, but unless you want to make that your career, be very careful with the partnerships you do make. Because if you start only sharing brand-promoting content, you might lose credibility as an expert in your space.

Give to get

The more you invest in your community and network and the more you give them for free, the more you will receive. I don't gatekeep any of my knowledge – I give it *all* away. In doing so, I get *ten times* as much back. The more you do for other people, the more comes back to you. Call it the law of attraction, gratitude, whatever you like. But in my experience, the more grateful you are for your audience and the more willing you are to share everything you know to benefit other people for free, the more money you will make.

People like and trust you more when you give your knowledge and expertise away for free, which means they will be more likely to pay you for your services. People want to do business with people they like and trust. Remember how I said that people love to spend money, but we all *hate* being sold to? *Giving* has the opposite effect. The more you give people, the more likely they are to give back. The formula that I think works is: give, give, give, give, give, give, give, then ask.

Stay humble

As you build this brand, grow this following, go viral, get recognised (that actually happens to me sometimes now, and it never doesn't freak me out), it's so important to stay humble. I learned the hard way how easy it is to get carried away when everything feels like it's going right – but the old saying 'pride comes before a fall' is true. And your ego bruises very easily.

At the start of 2023, Klowt had been named among the fastest-growing start-ups in London and I remember thinking, 'We've made it.' We were generating more revenue monthly than we ever had, and our growth was on trajectory for 270% year-on-year, which even for a start-up was quick. And then it all went wrong. I had a lot going on in my personal life, a divorce, a pretty toxic relationship, juggling being a single mother, the business and co-parenting. I wasn't in a good place – and so the business wasn't either. I hired too fast, the wrong people, didn't give them the training and the support they needed and we lost business, and employees as a result. It's funny how when you think you've cracked it, life humbles you. And it hurts. It hurts to know that you've let people down, or that you haven't done your best. But I'm so grateful for the experience, because it served me an ice-cold platter of self-awareness that after three years of mammoth growth and only wins, I really probably needed.

Gary Vee always says, 'I don't listen to the boos.' What he means is that he doesn't listen to the trolls, haters or the losses, which is important because they can seriously dent your confidence. But I'd add you *also* have to make sure you also don't listen to all the people who are telling you you're amazing. Because listening to them can have just as much of a destructive impact on your ego as the ones telling you you're not.

You have to reach a point where you can read all of those comments, hear people's words – good and bad – and not let them have an impact on you. I make a point of reading both. Earlier in my journey the negative comments might have turned me into a blubbering ball of anxiety, and the positive ones blew smoke up my fragile-ego-ass. Now? I'm indifferent. I take them for what they are. I know people telling me I'm fat, or ugly, or that I'm wrong even, say those things for a reason. Some with genuine challenge to my ideologies, and others with only a projection of their own insecurities. I'm grateful that people want to comment on and interact with my content, whether it's nice or not. Because either way, it's helping my brand grow. And the negativity in many ways reassures me that what I'm doing is the right thing, while keeping my head firmly on my shoulders.

And the negativity – of which you will get very little, I promise – has built a resilience in me that I hope this book will help you build too. My goal is to empower you to take control of your personal brand, but a magical byproduct of doing so is the resilience and confidence you develop within yourself. This confidence comes from learning to love your opinion of yourself more than you care about other people's opinions of you. And, therefore, you become immune to whether people like you or not – the place where old people on their deathbed wish they could have gotten to when they were younger. What a gift.

Honestly, as long as you're happy and excited about the content you share, the ideas you have, the places you want to see and the people you want to meet, who cares what anyone else thinks about it? Seriously, we're all going to die at some point, why would you waste a second of your life worrying about other people's opinions that have absolutely nothing to do with you? You have to train yourself to emotionally detach from the outcome of your content – even 12 months before writing this book I would get upset if one of my posts was misunderstood. But the more you focus on your own journey and your own ambitions and goals, the easier it is to let go of any negativity you experience online. Besides, engagement is engagement.

Remember, life isn't a popularity contest. And neither is your personal brand. As long as you're clear on your goal, who you need to attract to make that goal happen and bring those people on a journey with you by creating resonance, who cares if a handful of people on TikTok don't like your shirt?

Have fun

Every year I pick a word instead of a resolution, and this year for me was all about intentional fun. OK, two words. But I've spent the last four years of my life in survival mode. Hustling my little butt off to grow a business, and a personal brand, all while trying to navigate a divorce, co-parenting, keeping fit, maintaining a decent social life – and staying hydrated. Small violin, please. But there's a point in that – if it's not fun, don't post it. If the speaking gig is making you uncomfortable because it's new, just f**king go for it. But if you've been doing them for a while and you hate every second of doing it, why are you subjecting yourself to that madness? Taking control of your personal brand allows you to take control of your life, but if you're not enjoying what you're doing, that's now a you problem.

Of course, not everything will be fun. Sometimes creating content will feel like a chore. A tick box exercise – yes, it does happen. Sometimes you'll have bad days. You'll get booked for a podcast or speaking gig and on the day think, 'Why did I do this?' – but every time you do, it's amazing. And every post you share adds to your reputation, and your personal brand. I feel incredibly fortunate that *even ten people* care about what I have to say. So when I'm standing in front of an audience of several hundred people, it is unbelievably humbling.

I guess what I'm saying is that when people listen to you, you have a responsibility to deliver value for them, sure – but to enjoy doing it, because if not, you're wasting their time *and yours*.

Click moments

Approach your personal brand from a position of *giving*. Give your knowledge, your time and your energy away for free, and you'll get a much higher ROI than any amount you'd be paid.

Opportunities to monetise your personal brand will come along, and when they do, ask for your worth, and say it with your chest. Just as you and your personal brand evolve, so too will how you monetise your brand, and how you charge for your voice in a room. It's just a part of this process. But always come back to the value exchange – what value do you add for the other party, and what value do they add to you?

12

The future of branding is personal

As I write this book at the beginning of a new year (2024), I have a prediction to make. I reckon this year is the year of renaissance of in-person relationship building – that if you genuinely want to build a personal brand that will stand the test of time and deliver the career-defining opportunities you think you deserve, you have to be willing to do things in real life.

And, yes, social media still matters – but talking on stages, appearing on podcasts, grabbing random coffees, meeting in-person are going to mean so much more. Because with the rise of AI, and the mass adoption of social media as the only distribution channel that matters for brand building, in-person matters more than ever. If we look back through the history of marketing and branding – even in relation to products and services – every innovation stems back to one thing: community.

If you want to build resonance with people and for them to feel like they know you, you have to get to know *them* – and that's really hard to do if you limit yourself to only online interactions. It's like dating, who the hell wants to build a relationship over the phone? I don't – I want to meet you, see you, look you in the whites of your eyes. My advice, if you really want to accelerate the growth of your personal brand? Find a reason to go to in-person events or meet-ups where you can shake people's hands and have face-to-face conversations. Get their business cards. Use the real-life event to have an excuse to connect with people on social media, not the other way around. Be a real person who builds a real community.

The old adage of 'It's not what you know, but who you know' isn't true any more – it's all about *who knows you*. And it is really difficult for people to get to know you if you're not willing to build those relationships with those people, in person.

You can't outsource your personality to AI

I love ChatGPT. I love it for giving me content ideas, condensing information that I need to know, giving me the structure for how to write an engaging book! But I hate it for writing content. It's so obvious when AI has been used to create content these days – the tone is wrong, the voice is wrong – it's just weird. And it doesn't matter how sophisticated it becomes, a robot can never truly mimic a person. And that gives you a huge advantage.

Learn how to leverage AI to inform your content creation. Use it for things like providing you with suggested talking points on a given topic, compiling a list of the top ten trends in your industry, viral content previously posted on a topic or telling you what the leading search terms are on a given topic. Those are all things that, when done manually, are time-consuming – and whether you've done them manually or not makes very little difference to the content you create off the back of them.

And while all your competitors and peers are short-cutting their way to content creation by using the same tools to actually create their content, you're using it to inspire yours – so that you can create, as a human being, and tell the world your story. They sound like every other ChatGPT-created message, you sound like you. You automatically stand out, and you automatically win the biggest challenge of the year – attention.

Always remember that the point of personal branding is to create those human connections. Those connections come from authenticity. No bot could ever understand your story, the feelings you associate with it and everything you've been through in your life – so don't expect it to be able to produce relevant and engaging content about your experiences that will resonate with other real people. Think of AI as a tool that will facilitate your creativity and free up your time so you can spend time on what matters – connecting with people. But don't forget, you can't outsource your personality to AI.

The only way is up

Personal branding has become more and more mainstream (it's probably why you're reading this book) and yet it's still kind of taboo. Lots of people talk about it, but not that many people actually do it. Brands certainly aren't building it into their marketing strategies, despite success story after success story of founder brands driving company brand awareness (Ben Francis of GymShark).

This is where I think things will start to shift in the years after this book is published. I believe people will start to see personal branding as an integral distribution channel for marketing a business. People will realise that their personal brand is now their resume. Organisations will work out that unless their people are promoting their business, no one will care about it. It's a potent reintroduction of human-centred marketing that drives actual commercial results. And I can't bloody wait.

There is a huge void that *you* can fill with your experience, skills and life (if that's what you want to share) right now. There is a community of people waiting to hear from you. But the longer you leave it, the more you're going to be competing with other voices in your space – and the harder it's going to be to have yours heard.

The opportunity for you is huge. You have a strategy, you have the playbook. My mission is to inspire one million people to build their personal brand and be 100% OK with the consequences of being themselves. If I can build my personal brand around this goal as a single mum of two, who's also running a business, then so can you. Stop making excuses. Stop allowing fear, or timing, or lack of resources to dictate what your future will look like. Because that is what this is. Your future.

Taking control of my personal brand has given me opportunities I would never have dreamed of when I started – I own my own home, I drive a car I love, I can take my children on holidays. I have freedom. I DM'd Gary Vee in 2020 and told him how he'd inspired me to build my personal brand, and in 2024 I shared a stage with him and I got to talk to him about my business, my brand and my life. Building my personal brand changed my life. Now it's time to change yours.

Stop waiting for permission, and give it to yourself. Everything you want is out there available to you, you just need to reach for it. What the f**k are you waiting for?

Conclusion: just f**king post it!

Right at the beginning of this book, I told you about my goal with *The Personal Branding Playbook* was to help you take control of your personal brand – and your life. And if you have made it this far, you have everything you need to make that happen. Now it's up to you to make it happen.

That's the beauty of personal branding – it relies on *you*. You're not waiting for someone else to say you're good enough, or to give you a pay rise or to subtly tell you you're doing a good job. You're putting yourself out there and demanding all the opportunities you truly deserve, instead of waiting in the hope someone realises how brilliant you are and hands them to you on a plate.

But that also means the only thing standing in the way of success is, well, you. *You* have to commit to this journey. *You* have to put your big pants on. *You* have to just f**king post it.

I want you to pull out your phone, right now. Open up the notes section and I'm going to ask you a question, and I want you to answer this honestly – and, then, I want you to post it on social media. You could record yourself, write it – I don't care. But you need to post it.

Your first post

If you had only one moment left to live, and your action was to share a final message, what would your message be and why does that message mean something to you? End your post on 'the' lesson and ask other people to share theirs.

You've written your first post now. It's emotive. It's human. It will resonate with your audience. Now, hit 'post'.

And if you want people to see your first post? Add #justfckingpostit to the end. Every single person who has read this book will see that hashtag and celebrate your first little win.

Building your personal brand is simple.

Just f**king post it!

About the author

Amelia founded her first business at just 21 years old. Within 12 months of launching, Amelia's womenswear brand was stocked in 12 retailers and had large retailers like ASOS courting her to sell the clothes. In year two, Amelia lost everything. She was forced to close the doors on her business and that chapter in her life. Returning to the workforce, Amelia began a new career doing what she did best – sales.

As a tech headhunter, she quickly realised the quickest way to reach prospective clients was to market herself in the same way she marketed her business – using social media. This is where her journey into personal branding started. It wasn't long before people outside the organisation began noticing Amelia's content on LinkedIn and contacting her for help in building their personal brands online.

Now 33, Amelia has two children, a community online of over 250,000 people, a top 1% of downloads podcast, Branded, and has built a multi-million pound personal branding agency, Klowt, all on the back of her own personal brand. From serious early business failure to now creating a whole new category of marketing, Amelia's fast-growing personal branding agency, Klowt, has already made a dent in the space, operating on a 100% inbound model, working to build thought leadership and huge personal brands of leaders, founders and entrepreneurs globally.

Notes

Chapter 1

1. Amir, N. (2024) How to increase your vibration level by being authentic. 5 February. https://ninaamir.com/increase-vibration-level.

2. Freedman, M. (2024) Why word of mouth trumps traditional advertising. *Business News Daily*, 17 January. https://www.businessnewsdaily.com/2353-consumer-ad-trust.html

3. Pendell, B.R. (2022) Customer brand preference and decisions: Gallup's 70/30 principle. *Gallup.com*, 30 September. https://www.gallup.com/workplace/398954/customer-brand-preference-decisions-gallup-principle.aspx

Chapter 7

1. *Vogue Australia* (2018) The most inspiring Coco Chanel quotes to live by. *Vogue Australia*, 16 January. https://www.vogue.com.au/fashion/news/the-most-inspiring-coco-chanel-quotes-to-live-by/image-gallery/b1cb17be7e20734d0b255fbd5a478ed4

2. Vaynerchuk, G. *Jab, Jab, Jab, Right Hook: How to Tell Your Story in a Noisy Social World* (London: HarperCollins, 2013).

3. Apple (2001) Apple presents iPod. *Apple Newsroom*, 23 October. https://www.apple.com/newsroom/2001/10/23Apple-Presents-iPod/

Chapter 8

1. Statista (2023) Pizza Hut sales revenue in the United Kingdom (UK) 2012–2021. https://www.statista.com/statistics/913414/pizza-hut-sales-united-kingdom-uk/
2. Bradley, C. (2021) F1 fans becoming younger and more diverse, say Global Survey results. *motorsport.com*, 27 October. https://www.motorsport.com/f1/news/f1-fans-becoming-younger-and-more-diverse-say-global-survey-results-/6696732/

Chapter 9

1. Chierotti, L. (2021) Harvard professor says 95% of purchasing decisions are subconscious. *Inc.com*, 5 January. https://www.inc.com/logan-chierotti/harvard-professor-says-95-of-purchasing-decisions-are-subconscious.html
2. Freedman, M. (2024) Why word of mouth trumps traditional advertising. *Business News Daily*, 17 January. https://www.businessnewsdaily.com/2353-consumer-ad-trust.html

Chapter 11

1. Erskine, R. (2018) The key to increasing your brand's reach by 561%? Your employees. *Forbes*, 1 July. https://www.forbes.com/sites/ryanerskine/2018/06/30/the-key-to-increasing-your-brands-reach-by-561-your-employees/

Index